BAD TO THE BONE

"A real treat. Bo is so distinctively adorable and funny, that no other dog will be able to follow in his pawsteps."
>   —**Tracie Hotchner,** author of *The Dog Bible*
>   and host of *Dog Talk* (NPR affiliate
>   WLIU-FM 88.3 radio show)

"You'll laugh, you'll howl, you'll practically wag with pleasure . . . Bo is truly the voice of his doggy generation."
>   —**Dr. Marty Becker,** resident veterinarian on
>   ABC's *Good Morning America*, host of
>   *The Pet Doctor with Marty Becker* on PBS,
>   author of 17 pet books, nationally syndicated
>   columnist, and co-creator of petconnection.com

"A well-written and fun read . . . Bo takes you inside his family and you feel as if you're right there experiencing all the joys and pains with them. You'll want to hug your own dog after reading this book!"
>   —**Suzanne Jalot,** editor-in-chief of *DOGliving* magazine

"Bo's rebel adventures in naps and squirrels will stir the heart and stoke human understanding of how dogs must think. His 'voice' is utterly original, sharp, and kind."
>   —**Monica Collins,** "Ask Dog Lady"
>   columnist, www.askdoglady.com

"Witty commentary and hilarious o

D0030226

BAD TO THE BONE

BO HOEFINGER

Some days you're the dog,
Some days you're the hydrant.
I hope you enjoy my tail!
Woof Woof

CITADEL PRESS
Kensington Publishing Corp.
www.kensingtonbooks.com

CITADEL PRESS BOOKS are published by

Kensington Publishing Corp.
119 West 40th Street
New York, NY 10018

All Kensington titles, imprints, and distributed lines are available at special quantity discounts for bulk purchases for sales promotions, premiums, fund-raising, educational, or institutional use. Special book excerpts or customized printings can also be created to fit specific needs. For details, write or phone the office of the Kensington special sales manager: Kensington Publishing Corp., 119 West 40th Street, New York, NY 10018, attn: Special Sales Department; phone 1-800-221-2647.

CITADEL PRESS and the Citadel logo are Reg. U.S. Pat. & TM Off.

First printing: October 2009

10 9 8 7 6 5 4 3 2 1

Printed in the United States of America

Library of Congress Control Number: 2009930442

ISBN-13: 978-0-8065-3129-8
ISBN-10: 0-8065-3129-0

*This book is dedicated to all the shelter workers,
rescue groups and animal welfare proponents
who make this world better, one animal
at a time. You are unsung heroes and a
true inspiration.*

You restore my faith in humanity every day.

CONTENTS

CONTENTS

Preface

Let's get this clear right away: I'm a dog. I'm one-foot-ten and weigh sixty-three pounds, and although I'm a mutt on the outside, I'm a purebred on the inside. My good nature comes from the golden retriever side of the family, while my stubbornness is clearly from my chowchow bloodlines. I've got Rastafarian ears, a black tongue for licking, and paws that should be on a dog twice my size.

I type sixty words a minute.

My name is Bo.

I'm a senior dog. In fact, I'm in what God calls "bonus time." As any experienced dog will tell you, the desire to leave our urine stain on the proverbial fire hydrant of life grows stronger the longer the bond between you and owner exists. For me, the yearning is strong (sometimes as much as eleven times a day).

Some dogs memorialize themselves by using their teeth to carve their stories into the family furniture. Others prefer barking out an oral history. But I've always been a writer.

I usually do it in the snow, but for longevity sake, I've put paw to paper this time.

The unauthorized biography you hold in your paws was written without the express written consent of the two humans involved in these adventures. Seeing as owners never seem to ask their canines for permission when writing about them I extend the same discourtesy, at least until someone

leaves seven pounds of unmarked ground beef at a designated drop-off of my choosing.

I want to assure you, this book provides you with the
unique opportunity to share episodes in my life as they
unfolded, through the eyes of man's best friend. What you're
getting is 100 percent genuine Mr. Bo Hoefinger and family.
The characters in this book, the stories, and the thoughts are
all real. The names may have been changed to protect the
innocent.

So take pleasure in the world as I have seen it, experienced it, and lived it.

I welcome you to my mind and my story . . .

BAD TO THE BONE

Introduction

On a snowy Christmas Eve, less than ten days after I was rescued from an upstate N.Y. prison, I sat in front of a crackling fire surrounded by the two doting humans who had saved me. The male human began to tell a story, specifically the tale of why I was adopted. I listened intently, for surely there was wisdom behind his words.

"A long time ago, in the little town of Albany, lived a young woman. That woman, Bo, was your mother. She did her community work, was kind to others, and was always looking for a job. As you know, it took many years for her to find love, but she finally got her man and married him just eight months ago. That great man was me."

I saw him flash an adoring look at the woman in the room. I guess he hadn't yet realized he'd already bought the cow. Making goo-goo eyes at her wasn't going to get him more milk. He wasn't a dog, after all.

He continued. "As you can imagine there have been a lot of firsts over the past several months. The latest being the Christmas holiday. I was looking forward to it, but not as much as your mother. In fact she was so excited about decorating the Christmas tree, she could hardly contain herself."

I understood her excitement, for I enjoyed decorating trees, too. I suspect, though, my mother and I might have a difference of opinion on what one should use to decorate said Christmas tree.

My father carried on. "Unfortunately, on the day your mother decided to trim the tree, I had already made other arrangements to go out. Although I knew this did not sit well with her, I foolishly left to attend to my plans anyway.

"Your mother was so upset with this, it caused her to put in motion a most devious plan. A plan with long-term implications and one that would provide her companionship during the holiday season for years to come.

"That's right, Bo, her plan was to adopt a dog."

Well, at least now I knew who the smarter of the two is.

"When I returned from my errand late that night . . ."

My mother finally spoke up. "Tell him what the 'errand' was, honey."

In a lowered, sheepish tone he indulged her request. "When I returned from watching the football game with the guys, it was very cold in the house. Your mother didn't speak to me for two days.

"Just when I was beginning to think she'd never speak to me again, she called me at the office.

" 'Do you have anything you want to say to me?' she asked.

"I didn't know what to say so I didn't say anything at all. That's when I heard a dog bark in the background. So I asked your mother where she was.

"Your mother replied, and I might add, rather abruptly, 'I'm at the animal shelter. I'm adopting a dog to keep me company. You know, to provide me a little companionship, to help me around the house, to have something that I can count on. Some of the things I have been missing in my life.'

"Then she laid down the law, Bo. She said, 'So, if you want any input into what kind of dog we get, I suggest you get your butt over here. Otherwise, you'll just have to leave it up to me to pick out a good one.'

"Well the wheels of destiny had been set in motion. I raced to the shelter. Once I saw you, I knew you were the one."

He lowered his head, put it up against mine, and kissed me, as if to take credit for my release from canine prison.

I sat there, astounded by the story I had just heard.

There was no wise decision making behind adopting me. I wasn't chosen out of love, or to bring joy into someone's heart, as so many of my former cage mates had been. No, I was adopted as a reminder to my father that my mother, and her feelings, must always come first.

Simply stated, I was a revenge adoption.

Part One
In the Beginning . . .

CHAPTER 1

Of All the Gin Joints in
All the World . . .

We met back in the early '90s, December of '92 to be exact. I just had a major blowout with my first, somewhat dysfunctional family and decided that it was best for all if I just left. My foster dad gave me a ride to nowhere and before I knew it, I was at a boarding house in upstate New York. The place was great, warm with plenty of company, and their cheesy poof biscuits were to die for. On the downside, it was loud and smelly, not unlike me.

Even a lowly pug could smell her coming from miles away. It was Monday, as I recall, and the bells on the door jingled to announce her arrival. She was a beautiful blonde with a quick smile and a determined look. We'd seen this type before; they usually left with one of the pure-bred puppies, but something was different about this one. My instincts told me that any canine would be darn lucky to go home with a girl like her, so I made it my top priority to be that hound.

She wandered back to where we lived. Frankly, I was a bit embarrassed about the condition of the place. Some of my cage mates were not very clean and some even took to pooping where they ate. My next-cage neighbor's lack of etiquette was particularly noteworthy as he took to eating kitty snickers (that's slang for cat poo in the big house) openly. Sure they taste good, but you're not getting adopted if you're seen eating one.

As she came closer to my humble accommodations, I tried everything I could to grab her attention. When she finally got to me I made direct eye contact with her, tilted my over-sized cranium at a forty-five degree angle, and gave her my trademark BoPaw reach.

I could see instantly she wanted me. Needed me. Had to have me. Hey, who wouldn't?

She reached out and petted me with her finely manicured nails. She was clearly enjoying our encounter. How easy these humans are to manipulate, I thought. Her hands were refreshingly cool and her smell put me in a state of delight. I was in love. I could tell she loved me, too.

After a few gushing, "He's so cute!" comments, she gave me one last look and proceeded on to Pumpkin's cage.

Realizing I was still sitting there with a half-cocked head and a paw in the air, I felt my muzzle glow red hot under my furry face as the other dogs chuckled with delight. *Hey lady, we just made a connection. You can't move on. Our story ends here if you keep going.* But that's exactly what she did. By the time I regained my bearings, she had moved through the room, out the door, and out of my life.

My hope for a better life was gone as quickly as it had come. The brief glimpse of a finer existence with a loving, caring human was replaced with the stark reality that I might spend the rest of my life at this boarding house. What was once a fun and refreshing place became a dark and daunting cave.

I admit this brush with love, and the subsequent loss of it, had me thinking of ending things in this world. I had heard the stories of the different ways to get to rainbow bridge, but I knew that if I were going to get there, there was only one canine to whom I could turn.

His given name was Charlemagne Brutus the IV, but he was better known in the big house as the Candyman. His studded dog collar betrayed an otherwise noble and tame appearance. He was well connected, and his lifestyle was proof of that. C'man slept on the best blankets, drank from the shiniest bowls, and rarely took to begging for human food.

I approached Candyman during exercise time in the yard. While the other dogs were working on their begging routines, he let on to me that he had a shipment of Hershey's dark chocolate candy bars on the way. For the right price he would let me have them. I knew, as did he, chocolate will kill a canine quicker than a game of "chase the cat" in traffic. Yeah, that quickly.

Death by chocolate, as it is commonly referred to in the restaurant business, was only two Hershey's bars away for me. Once ingested, I would soon be patrolling the pearly gates of heaven, looking, of course, for a place to dig out. Paradise awaited me.

But the price was steep; a greenie and a peanut butter–filled Kong for the candy bars. I had no money and I was unemployed, so I resigned myself to the situation at hand. At least death would come seven times faster than it does for others on this lonely, desolate planet.

I lowered my already slouched body onto the well worn blanket covering the cage's tin floor. Surely there was another way out of this situation.

I lay there, thinking about my options. Maybe during exercise time I could climb the fence and escape? I would be free again. The trouble was the shelter workers were on high alert ever since Hairy Houdini, the border-collie mix, escaped last month. Maybe I could steal the German shepherd's treats. Surely, once Ruger found out, he'd give me the business end of a chewy shiv. Hmmm, that sounds a little too painful.

Maybe if I . . .

I lay there for hours, searching for a solution. When I finally fell asleep, the perfect escape was still out of my paws' grasp.

Upon awakening, an angel stood over me. The very same blond angel that had visited me earlier in the day. Next to her was a very handsome young man. So handsome you might think he was gay, but let me assure the reader he is not. He looked at me and said, "He's cute. Let's get him."

"I want you to look at this one over here, too," the angel countered.

What? Another dog? She's betraying me all over again. It was Christmas season, and I felt just like a Douglas fir being picked up, manhandled, and then tossed aside in favor of a bigger, better tree.

Fortunately the man had his wits about him. "No, I like this one, he's so dopey looking. We don't need to look at any of the others. He's the one." I didn't much care for his attitude but his decision-making capability was flawless.

The attendant, known as Nurse Ratchet by the inmates, lingered nearby. She was eager to get rid of me after my failed attempt at unionizing the locals to get better victuals. "Would you like to take him out for a walk, just to make sure you like him?" she offered, knowing full well that once prospective parents take a dog for a "test" walk, they will adopt the pet 98 percent of the time.

Once outside, I made a beeline for my potential owner's car. It was easy to pick out; my sense of smell is incredible. In a show of respect I immediately peed on the front driver's side tire. The couple tried to fawn all over me, but I ignored them. Once you have them this far, you show them you don't want them and they'll want you more.

Remember, don't hate the player; hate the game.

The ploy worked like a charm; while they informed Ratchet they wanted me, I pranced back toward my former home to pack my belongings.

"Not so fast my friend," Ratchet cackled. "We need to make sure you get all your required shots before we can release you to these fine folks."

What do you mean I can't leave yet? What a shot in the nads, which by the way were already gone. My new parents were told to come pick me up later in the week.

As they went to put me back in my cage, I abandoned my "good boy" act and did my best to stop this course of action. I sat down and refused to move, forcing two, it might have been three, of the staff's goons to drag me across the floor and into lockdown. As they dragged me away, I got one last look at my new owners, who stared at the commotion with shocked looks that said, "What have we gotten ourselves into?"

It's a look they would share many times in our future together.

My Favorite Quotes

(As Written by the Author's Dog)

 Never worry about the size of your Christmas tree. In the eyes of your dogs, they are all 30 feet tall fire hydrants.
—Wee Willy Wilde; Larry Wilde's heavy-drinking Lab

 Whatever the mind can conceive and believe, the mind can achieve. Now, watch as I make my father say no to that last meatball and give it to me.
—Slacker, Dr. Napoleon Hill's overachieving coon hound

 Neither a lofty degree of intelligence nor imagination nor both together go to the making of genius. Love, love, love, that is the soul of genius. And I love, love, love the Iams Savory Sauce on my food. Now that's genius.
—Tone Deaf, Mozart's collie, great-great-great-uncle of Tone Loc

 You can have everything in life that you want if you just give enough other people what they want. I've given plenty of people more than enough attitude to get me everything I want, even an iPhone with a two-year contract.
—Stingy, Zig Ziglar's tight-pawed Yorkie

Great works are performed, not by strength, but by perseverance. That's how one is able to knock over the garbage pail, eat its contents, and leave the remnants all over the house.
—Hercules, Samuel Johnson's diminutive Chihuahua

Whether you think you can or whether you think you can't, you're right! Evidence that proves canines are never wrong.
—Pinto, Henry Ford's wise but explosive bull terrier

You see things; and you say "Why?" But I dream of things that never were; and I say "Why not?" and I wonder "Why not dig under the fence and run free?"
—George Bernard Paw, Mr. Shaw's big-mitted best friend

Never look down on anybody unless you're helping him up. Or licking his face.
—Smooches, Jesse Jackson's pit bull

Even if you are on the right track, you will get run over if you just sit there. A lesson that you should always be careful when an owner commands you to sit.
—A-Train, Will Rogers's single-minded boxer

CHAPTER 2

Homecoming

It was a long two days as I awaited the return of the angel to take me home with her. I smelled her before I saw her. She was close, front lobby close, and before I knew it, the loudspeaker blared, "Cage eight for pick up."

Cage 8, that was me! Sure, I was being treated no better than a Grand Slam breakfast at Denny's, but hey, at least I wasn't going to be served up to some drunken college kids.

I packed my belongings, said my final good-byes, and with a leash around my neck, sprinted for the door.

She was just as pretty as I remembered, and she smelled even better. She had an engaging smile with nice white teeth. They weren't Bugs Bunny big or Rocky the Squirrel small, but just the right size. Looking at her, I guessed she was roughly four years old and couldn't have weighed over a hundred and five soaking wet.

This was my new mother.

She took the leash and led me outside and to the beginning of a most memorable life.

On the ride home she never stopped smiling, constantly alternating her stare between the road and me. I knew if I played this right, the unconditional love coming my way could be used to my advantage. I sensed it was going to be easy. Very easy.

That said, I still had to be careful. People were a fickle breed. If I jumped back and forth in the car too much, or a burp was erroneously construed as a growl, or even if an inadvertent fart squeaked by the goalie so early in the game, the tide of goodwill could turn against me.

I sat upright in the passenger seat, looking forward, doing my best to "mirror" her behavior. When we stopped at one particular light, I noticed a car next to us filled with kids. They were pointing at me and trying to get my attention, but I ignored them like they were the paparazzi. Out of the corner of my eye, I could see my mother laughing at my actions.

"You really think you're a person, don't you?"

Hey, if it gets me out of a cage and into a warm bed, sure. Heck, I'd be willing to play a cat to get that. Okay, maybe not a cat, but you catch my drift.

To seal the deal I employed one of the most powerful tools available to canines riding in cars; it's called the "lean-in." No human in the history of dog/owner relations has ever been able to speak negatively of their dog after experiencing it.

As the car turned left, I leaned in toward my mother. I mean, really leaned in, until my ears pressed against her shoulder. I kept leaning until my head slipped from her shoulder and into her lap.

My mother laughed and petted my head.

It was official, she was mine.

After what seemed to be an eternity, we pulled into a driveway in front of a small, two-story mustard-colored house. No, not classic mustard yellow, but Gulden's Spicy Brown. I noted to myself: landscaping in front could use some help.

My mother secured my leash and opened her car door. Almost immediately, the cabin of the vehicle filled with a mixture of odors. It was overwhelming, and although I much preferred the new owner smell that preceded it, I was compelled to find the source.

I jumped across the seat, onto her lap, and spring-boarded my way to the outside world. As soon as my paws hit the cold driveway, I was off like a rocket. I could practically taste my freedom, when my head snapped backward; I had reached the end of the leash, onto which my new mother was holding fast. Hmm . . . she was stronger than she looked.

After I got over my humiliation, she led me around the yard so I could smell the surroundings. My new home was squeezed in between two other, non–condiment-colored houses. Welcome to suburbia, I thought. This sure beat the cramped quarters of the city and its concrete playground. Sure I'd miss the easy access to the theater district, but at least I wouldn't be badgered to "go poopie" in a hidden stairwell.

With the skill of an urban graffiti artist, I left an artistic "Bo Lives Here" message in the front yard. Moments later I made my way to the back of the house, looking to create another work of art.

When I turned the corner, what I saw purt' near put a tear in my eye. For what lay in front of me was a vast expanse of unexplored woods. No houses, no roads, no people. Just trees, bushes, and yes, oh yes, a creek. In law circles it's called "forever wild." In canine circles it's called a dog park. There was so much to explore, I couldn't wait for my chance to do it "off leash."

Next, she led me through the front door, across a tiny foyer, and into the kitchen. Say good-bye to the 1990s, and say hello to the 1970s. This place was decked out in Hershey-brown cabinets, yellow appliances, and a Dating Game flowery linoleum floor. Not really my style, but if Tiger from the Brady Bunch could handle this type of décor, well so could I.

My mother and I stood there in the kitchen. I looked up at her. She looked down at me. After a few moments of awkward silence, it was apparent my mother didn't know what to do. Finally, she tied my leash around the dishwasher handle and sat down at what I'll charitably call the kitchen table. Others, with less tact, would call it a card table. There she sat, looking at me and smiling. And there I sat, looking back at her and scheming.

How should I slip this collar off? When should I do it? How fast is she? What was a big plant doing inside a house? When should I water it? . . .

The thoughts just kept coming and wouldn't stop. At last my mother got up and left the room, reappearing with a blanket and a handful of dog toys. She placed the armful of stuff on the family room floor, which was conveniently located off the kitchen, then she released me from the dishwasher and coaxed me to join her.

"Come here, Bo. Lay down on the blanket. C'mon buddy."

My first instinct was to blow her off and go check out the freshness of the toilet water, but I thought it better to do as she said and feel out the situation. I lay down on the cushy blanket and perused the plastic doggie newspaper that was part of the potpourri of toys strewn about. It was an old paper; Nixon was still president. My mother took the opportunity to lay down behind me and started petting my head. Having been yelled at and abused for most of my eleven months on this planet, I hadn't experienced this kind of unconditional love. Heck, I didn't even know it existed until this very moment. The best part about it was that it was a two-way street. It felt good, and right. I had just finished the sports section, when a loud grinding noise filled the air. It came from outside the living room door. It was the first time I'd ever heard a garage door opening, and to this very day, it's a sound that gets my juices flowing.

"Your father's home!" my mother squealed.

Seconds later the door opened into the living room and in walked the hero from the dog pound.

I guessed he was about the same age as my new mother. He sported a Fred Flintstone five o'clock shadow, stood about six feet tall, and displayed average girth. If you smelled him in a crowd, you wouldn't notice him. Even though he appeared average, I suspected his size would allow him to control me on a leash, unlike my skinny mother.

His eyes widened when he saw me and he quickly approached, staring directly at me the whole time. This move would have been unsettling under any circumstance, but was even more enhanced by his rather menacing unibrow. Was this a power move on his part, or was he just clueless? Hadn't he ever gone to doggie body language school? When I met his challenge and growled at him, he quickly averted his eyes and backed down. Bo: 1, new father: 0. I made a mental note: "don't fear the unibrow—it's not as scary as it looks."

After giving my mother a quick kiss, he sat down and we all just lay there for the next few hours on the floor. They petted me and fed me, told me I was cute and smart, and basically doted on my every move. Every human should have it so good. That's right, I said human.

When it was time to go to bed, we walked up the tiny steps to the bedroom. Upon walking in I spotted the place where I would sleep. No, not on the floor, or the dog bed, but rather on top of that big old mattress, and smack dab in the middle of the two well-worn spots where my parents slept.

Here I lay, after the most wonderful day I had ever experienced, thinking about the fortuitous change in my life.

It was obvious my new parents were a couple in need of canine companionship, and who better to bond with than me? But, truth be told, we all got what we needed. They needed something to love besides themselves and I needed to be loved.

I rolled over and stretched my legs, pushing my mother to the edge of the bed. Ahh, much better. This could be a fun life after all, as long as these humans proved trustworthy. Based on my previous encounter with humans and a home, this was still up for debate.

I woke up the next morning, momentarily confused by the softness of my bed and the quietness of my surroundings. I certainly wasn't in Kansas anymore. Much to my delight, I lay between two bodies, both of which were awake and gazing at me.

Their constant staring made me a bit self-conscious. Did I have a booger hanging out of my nose? Was my fly unzipped? No, it was just the fact that I was so darned cute. What can I say, I hit the gene pool lottery.

"Bo, !@%TDD$%@#$FDF?" my mother asked. Loosely translated that means, "Bo, you gotta whiz?"

Of course I did . . . and so day two of my new life began.

CHAPTER 3

Nobody's Perfekt

It wasn't long before we settled into a routine. My father would leave early in the morning and not come back home until late at night. My mother was unemployed, and therefore with me throughout the day. We took a lot of trips around town together. She was also the one who took me on my morning and noon walks, and joined my father and me on the evening ones.

It was the evenings that were especially joyous to me. After taking a long walk, the family would sit down in front of the fireplace and watch television. One night I'd be *Hangin' with Mr. Cooper* while the next I'd be patrolling the dusty plains of America with *Walker, Texas Ranger*. Throughout the evening I would get bones to chew on, plates to lick, and toys to ignore.

If only Candyman could have seen me: I lived in a house, slept in a warm bed, and owned two human food dispensers. I had it all, and at a very young age.

But things can change in a heartbeat.

During one blustery evening while my father was away on a business trip, my mother and I lay on the floor of the living room watching the latest episode of *Seinfeld*.

After a good licking of my paws, I rolled over to expose my belly. My mother took the opportunity to give me a full frontal body massage. Her technique differed from my father's in that she rubbed certain areas more often than others. I thought to myself, C'mon honey, it's like suntan lotion, spread it evenly.

Oddly, the more I relaxed, the more she tensed up. After she finished, she stood up and paced about the room. So much for basking in the afterglow of a good rubdown, her rambling back and forth on the hardwood floor was making me anxious.

On the comment card, I was forced to give it three paws out of five.

When the telephone rang, she pounced on it. I could tell from her tone that she was speaking to my father, but something about the quiver of her voice made the fur on the back of my neck stand up. "Honey," she said, "I think there's something wrong with Bo."

Uh-oh.

After a brief silence, she continued. "I can't be sure but I think he has cancer."

Even I could here my father's response through the phone: "What?!"

"I gave him a massage tonight and I felt these lumps on his chest." She was in a near panic now. "And the thing is . . . the thing is . . . they didn't stop there. They were on his stomach, too. I think it's spread all over him."

She fell silent, listening to my father's advice, then said, "I agree. I'll get him to the vet first thing tomorrow. I love you," and hung up the phone.

Silence filled the room, giving me a moment to contemplate the severity of the situation. I felt fine, I really did. When I licked myself, like the vet tells you to, I hadn't noticed any aberrations at all. This thing called cancer is a silent killer, I thought, because there wasn't any outward evidence of it.

Naively, I believed humans were superior beings and

knew better than me. If my mother was this worried, surely something was very wrong.

Clearly, I had a lot to learn.

After a sleepless night, we readied ourselves to go to the veterinarian's office. I had been up all night thinking about the Big C. My mother looked worried, too, but neither of us made any mention of the reason for the appointment.

We arrived at the clinic moments after 9:00 a.m., and the room was already full of owners and pets. My mother and I signed in, squeezed between two owners sitting on a bench, and waited our turn.

Thoughts of my impending diagnosis filled my head when I heard the young receptionist ask the roomful of folks, "Is Bee-Oh in the room?"

My mother and I looked to the right and then to the left. We looked around the whole room, as did every other living thing, thinking the same thing, *"Who would name their pet Bee-Oh?"* Maybe it was the Japanese looking owner sitting in the corner of the room?

Once again we heard, "Is Bee-Oh here?"

When no one responded, the teenage helper checked the chart. "Hoefinger. Bee-Oh Hoefinger. Is he or she here?"

My mother's ears perked up as she realized what the young lady had been trying to say.

"Uhmm, do you mean Bo?"

Trying to hide her embarrassment the girl just said, "Uhh, yes. The vet will see you now."

Great. As if having a life-threatening illness wasn't bad enough, I was now an acronym for body odor. I rolled my eyes and told the girl to just talk to the paw.

Admittedly it came out sounding a lot like, "Woof, woof."

We were directed to the second sitting room where we awaited the arrival of my primary care physician.

Thoughts continued to bounce around in the cavern of my brain. Life couldn't be so cruel as to give me a home and a doting family, only to snatch it away, could it? I vowed to get a second opinion, especially if the diagnosis on my chart was spelled Kancer.

After quite some time, the vet opened the door and came in. He was tall and skinny, and he wore a white lab coat.

As this was the first time my mother required the services of a pet doctor—I had only been with the family for a month— she had many questions for him. I had some, too.

The first was, "Where are my balls?" and the second was, "Can I have them back?"

Before I could even open my mouth to ask, my mother began firing questions at him. After some time he was able to assure her that he was a licensed practitioner in the state of New York and that he was up to speed on all things dog. This seemed to calm my mother down, although the fresh smell of his diploma on the wall made me uneasy.

Quickly thereafter my mother told him of the lumps all over my chest and stomach. The more she talked the more hysterical she got.

This prompted Dr. Feelgood to grope me all over. After a few strokes here, a pat there, and an inappropriate touch later, the doctor said he couldn't find a thing. I felt like telling him to leave a twenty-dollar bill on the table for the good time, but before I could he asked my mother to point out what she had felt.

She quickly found the first lump, a second, and then a third. There were more and they were everywhere. I was as good as dead . . . three weeks, maybe a month to live by my estimation. I'd never have the opportunity to pee on a Frenchman in Paris, to sniff an Italian crotch at the Vatican, or to outwit a Polack in Warsaw.*

---

*I'm just kidding . . . I love the French, especially for their bread; I love the Italians, especially for their crime organization skills; I love the Polish, especially for the ability to change a lightbulb in groups.

I rolled glumly toward the doc so he could verify the prognosis.

He confirmed my mother's fears, "You're right. There are growths all over his body."

I waited for the fateful words to pass his lips, "I'm sorry, but Bo has cancer," but they never came.

In fact, according to the doc, they weren't cancerous at all. "What you're feeling there ma'am, are called nipples. Dogs, both female and *male*, have them all over their bodies. You did know that male dogs have nipples, didn't you?"

"It's not cancer, then?" my mortified mother asked.

"Uhmm, no," the doctor said. And then with a small laugh he asked, "Did you know men have nipples, too?"

"I'm not an idiot. Of course I knew that!" my mother responded, although in the back of my mind I wondered if she really did.

As he left the room, the doctor gave my mother some final words of wisdom: "Oh, if you're wondering what that big growth is at the base of his belly, that's a penis."

With that and a wink, he was gone, not only out of the room but as my primary care physician as well.

After the door shut, I jumped up and down with relief. I had my life back. I had my life back! My mother, however, stood there like a cigar store Indian, trying to make sense of what just transpired.

I quickly came to realize some humans were superior beings after all. It's just that my mother wasn't one of them.

Even though the day started out ominously, it ended with no enduring consequences. Well, none other than the annual mammograms my mother now has me get.

CHAPTER 4

Twisted Sister

They met, quite by chance, at my father's apartment. Both my parents had just graduated college and were looking to enjoy a final summer of freedom. As luck would have it, my father's roommate was dating my mother's friend. And thus it transpired that a casual stop by my father's apartment turned into a lifelong romance.

As my father tells it, he was immediately impressed with her and, being the go-getter that he is, ignored her. He was of the school, pay no heed to them and they'll want you more. That's probably why he spent the majority of his college years standing next to a keg, by himself.

As my mother tells it, he was just a shy guy on the couch who wouldn't say boo, but he was cute in a quiet kind of way.

Destiny would provide for several more chance encounters throughout the summer, allowing them to get to know each other. After a street festival filled with drinks, my father finally got up the nerve to ask her out.

Their first dinner was at Margarita's, their first movie *Crocodile Dundee*, and their first kiss was in an apartment overlooking a Dunkin' Donuts. If it was me, I would have passed on the kiss and opted for an apple fritter instead. The important thing was that my parents had found each other, and in the process someone they could each count on when times got tough.

Now, many years later, they were completing the first year of their marriage and getting to know me—their first dog.

Over the few months I'd been with them, I noticed they had a loving relationship. They didn't show it in traditional ways like licking each other, or smelling each other's crotch, but rather by giving a pat on the rear here and a smooch there. With some people you can just tell they were made for each other.

As a rule, I didn't generally trust humans, although these two were tough to resist. Take for instance my mother. Although I wasn't sure why she wasn't working, it allowed us to take many walks, go on spur of the moment car rides, or just lay around watching TV during the day. I loved the feel of her hand on my head, the sound of my name passing her lips, and the smell of her Chef Boyardee cooking. The tentacles of a lifelong bond started to grow.

The relationship with my father, on the other hand, was based on the games we played in the limited hours we spent together when he got home from work. Most notably we played tug-of-war. With my strong jaws, I won easily unless he cheated, which he often did by blowing in my face. Trust me, you would have let go of the rope, too—the man did not like to use Scope. Regardless, I'd still let him win every once in a while. It helped to boost his confidence and it brought us closer together.

All in all, things were progressing rather nicely and I was slowly letting my guard down.

It wasn't long, however, before my mother found work outside of the home and changed the dynamics of our routine.

She held a criminal justice degree and was eager to put it to use. Her opportunity came in the form of a paralegal

Top Ten Reasons
I Love My Mother

1. She feeds me.

2. She saved me from a life in the big house.

3. When I bark at her, she'll bark back.

4. She falls for my hard of hearing routine.

5. She's a sucker for the doe eye look.

6. She feeds me.

7. She lets me sleep on the bed.

8. She lets me sit in the passenger seat.

9. She has the patience of a saint.

10. She feeds me.

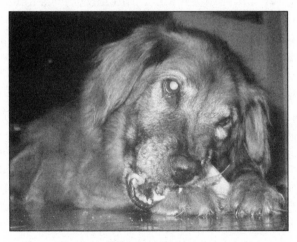

T-Bone = Love

position for a real estate attorney. Her primary job duties were to file this, copy that, and collate it all until her head hit the desk. If her doing this wasn't a crime, she didn't know what was, but it helped pay the bills. At least for a few weeks, anyway.

The downside was that I was now alone during the day. Sure my mother would try to break free at lunch to feed me and let me do my duty outside, but it just wasn't the same as before.

Life became boring, especially during the long stretches of "me" time I now had. Let's face it, there's only so much furniture and shoes one can chew on before it gets dull. Yeah, you can throw in a precious collectible to spice things up a bit, but the real action doesn't start until the family comes home. That's why I was pleased to hear my parents discussing the possibility of adding another player to the game of life, Bo's Life.

In an effort to explain away some of my recent bad behavior to my father, my mother told him, "He's lonely. That's why he keeps chewing the leg on the couch."

"I don't know. I think he's doing it out of spite," he said. "I mean look at what he did to that Barbara Woodhouse training book I got. No bad dogs, my ass."

"Remember, he just started the chewing thing since I went to work. I think if we got him a companion, he'd settle down and become less stubborn."

"I don't think we're ready for another dog. We can't even handle this one."

Giving it some thought my mother offered, "How about a cat? They're low maintenance and Bo can play with it during the day."

"A cat? I'm not really that keen on cats."

"What do you have against cats?"

"I don't know. I guess it's that they don't do much. They

lay around sleeping all day, only getting up long enough to eat."

Huh. Not unlike my father on a weekend.

Over the years, my father had developed a tainted view of felines that began with his boyhood cat, Ooshie. At the age of eleven he mistook the awful sounds of Ooshie having "sexy time" late one night for fighting. He rushed into his parents' room and woke his father, begging him to save Ooshie. By the time they got to the scene, Ooshie lay on her back smoking a cigarette, clearly satisfied with her encounter, thus giving my young, innocent father his first lesson of the Birds and the Bees.

Stranger still was my mother's willingness to get a cat. You see, she was actually afraid of cats. What caused this fear was anyone's guess, but rest assured, in the deep, dark recesses of her mind, a boogeyman cat lounged about. I'm not talking about a big mountain lion or leopard or even lynx-size cat, but a regular, run of the mill house cat. That's why I have to give her credit for showing such bravery, and all just for little ole fuzzy me.

But it wasn't a done deal yet. The conversation continued over the course of several days, and it became clear that I needed to do something to expedite the decision. A box of chewed baseball cards strewn about the guest bedroom did the trick quite nicely.

My mother turned to her sister, Marcy, for support in moving forward with the decision. Marcy owned so many cats that, had she not been married, she would have been referred to as the cat lady of her neighborhood. Fortunately, marriage to her husband, Jon, saved her from that fate. Today, neighbors simply call them the cat couple. Marcy had plenty of feline experience and my mother was determined to tap into it for my benefit.

It began with a long telephone conversation between my

mother and Marcy outlining the pros of owning a cat. My mother did most of the listening. By the time she hung up, she was excited to find me a partner.

"Bo, we're getting you a cat!"

That enthusiasm didn't last long, for on the day of the adoption, I could smell the fear emanating from my mother's pores. It was cat-induced fear, and once you smell that, you never forget it. Fortunately she was still committed to following through on her promise.

She left early that morning and I sat patiently, waiting for her return.

Hours later, the grind of the garage door's gears signaled the action was about to begin. I sprang from the floor, ran to the door, and barked with anticipation at meeting my new housemate.

The door opened slowly and in walked my mother, clutching a gray-striped tiger cat. That cat didn't know it yet, but she was about to inherit the bottom spot of the Hoefinger household pecking order. No doubt, a position my mother was happy to relinquish.

I jumped up to get a good whiff of the cat's behind, only to receive a quick right cross from her tiny kitty paw. Interesting. This cat was a fighter and a female one at that.

"Bo. No! Down! Down!" my mother shrieked.

Not deterred, I jumped up once more only to receive another swat across the face.

"No jump! Down! Leave it!"

My mother was trying every command in the book. Hadn't she realized I'd chosen not to learn any of them yet?

All this commotion was too much for the feline. She extended her claws, scratched my mother's arm, and jumped to freedom.

My mother screamed, the cat hit the ground running, and not to be outdone, I gave chase.

After a frenzied tour of the house, my new sister chose the living room couch to hide under. Trying not to provoke the situation anymore, I took a disciplined approach to getting close. I put my nose to the floor (a sign of friendship) and inched up to the sofa, my nose getting closer with each scoot, until my head was finally under it. There she sat, staring back at me.

I gave her the "I'm here in peace and mean you no harm" look, followed by an almost imperceptible whine. It sounded pathetic, just as it was intended.

Before Moose could respond in kind, I was yanked backward and escorted to the upstairs bedroom by my mother. In the end, I gave in, but I didn't make it easy on her.

With my ear to the bedroom floor, I heard my mother coax the cat out from under the couch. Moments later, I was released.

I ran out of the bedroom, scoured the upstairs, searched the main floor, and looked in every nook and cranny in between. It wasn't until I heard a distant "Meow" that I realized the cat was in the basement, and out of my reach.

My mother wasn't taking any chances. The cat had already "attacked her" once, she probably thought the next assault would turn deadly. I'm sure her concern for me never entered the picture.

I had to wait until my father came home to get up close and personal with my sister.

In the meantime, my mother sat me down and told me of my new sibling's adoption.

"We met, your aunt Marcy and I, at the shelter. Even though I was a bit scared I was eager to get inside to look at the kittens.

"Don't let my eagerness fool you Bo; I didn't really want to have to pick one up because, really, what's to stop it from viciously attacking me? Certainly not your aunt, but I did want to see what the shelter had to offer.

"When I saw the cages, I thought it was best to have aunt Marcy take the cats out one by one, hold them, and if a battle to the death didn't ensue, make them a candidate on our adoption list.

"The very first feline Marcy picked up was this gray, tiger striped kitten about nine months old. She was average and there was really nothing to distinguish her from the rest of the cats, but she did pass the 'attack' portion of the interview. I told Marcy to put her back and to move on to the next one.

"Well, let me tell you, Bo, this cat did not like being passed over. Before letting us take two steps, she stuck her paw underneath the cage and started frantically pumping it in and out. If I didn't know better I would have thought she was giving your aunt and me the middle finger!

"I certainly couldn't ignore that, could I? So, I turned around and went back to take a closer look. She stared at me with unwavering eyes. I could tell she was strong willed and had quite an attitude."

Hmm . . . sounds like a dog I know.

"Well Bo, I made my decision right then and there. This cat was the one for us!"

Of course my mother never stopped to consider *my* needs. I would have preferred a weak-willed, gutless companion. Someone to do my bidding for me, if you will. But hey, having an additional personality around was still an improvement over the current situation.

My mother continued her story. "Remember how we had to wait to pick you up? Well, with kittens, you get to take them right away. I wasn't prepared for that, so I had to ask the shelter for a box to carry your new sister home in. We punched some holes in it, put the cat in, and closed the lid."

Wow, how undignified.

I also knew the humiliation didn't end there. You see, the vehicle my new sister was going to be taken home in was also a bit degrading. It was an orange 1981 Ford Mustang. This particular car wasn't one of those cool Mustangs you see in magazines but one of the worst cars ever built. It must have been built on a Friday, before a long weekend. Besides being an eyesore, this vehicle rattled like crazy, lacked power windows, and most importantly on this day, was without a working air conditioner.

Did I mention that it was orange?

"So I took the box, put it in the car, and bid Aunt Marcy good-bye. I was so excited to get the cat home to show her to you.

"It wasn't long into the trip when I heard this thumping noise from the back of the car. At first I thought it was a flat tire, but quickly realized it wasn't. I turned my head to look in the backseat, when, much to my horror, the top of the box popped open like a jack-in-the-box!

"But Bo, instead of a scary clown springing up, an angry cat jumped out!"

Man, I wish she would have invited me along for the ride. I'd have given up a week's worth of my unprovoked barking to see the look on her face when Freddy Krueger sprang to life.

She continued. "Well the windows were open because it was so hot . . . I really wish your father would get that a/c fixed . . . and the cat looked to jump through one of them.

"What could I do? I couldn't let her leap out of a moving vehicle and onto a major highway. I had no choice but to lunge for her. I was scared, but I caught her by the tail and reeled her in, all while negotiating traffic.

Wow, it's true what they say. Women do multitask very well.

"I gotta tell you, Bo, after I managed to pull the car over and get the windows closed, I didn't feel so afraid of her anymore. One thing is for sure your new sister doesn't like car rides like you do.

"You know how you like to sit in the passenger seat and look all cute? Well she likes to sit on my head, massage my hair, and meow at the top of her lungs. I bet it looks cute, but I really can't tell. And it's not the safest way to drive a car."

If anybody could pull off the kitty turban look, it was my mother.

"Well, after a forty-five-minute ride . . . here we are."

Just another average drama-filled day in the life of my mother. But she still hadn't answered my most burning question. I wagged my tail and gave her my best adorable look, but to no avail.

"Oh no, Bo, I'm not going to let the cat out of the cellar until your father comes home."

Seemed to me she was still scared.

She called Aunt Marcy to relay the news of her adventurous ride home. As I listened in, I picked up on a nugget of new information . . .

"Yes. We're going to call her Moose," said my mother.

Moose? Thank goodness I came pre-named into this family.

"Why Moose you ask? Because I wouldn't let my honey name her Cow."

Cats have nine lives, and with this family, Moose would need them all.

CHAPTER 5

Raising Arizona

My father arrived home several hours after my mother had locked up Moose in the basement. Upon learning of the cat's location, he quickly retrieved her and brought her into the living room.

With my father, the encounter with Moose was a bit more controlled and pleasant. He held Moose and allowed me to sniff her up and down. I let Moose sniff me as well. She wasn't what I had pictured in a cat. She was actually quite sociable and playful. I suppose you can't judge a book by its cover, even if it is covered in cat hair.

We slept in the same bedroom that first night, and for many thereafter. There wasn't going to be a Hatfield and McCoy lifelong battle between us, but rather one closer to Donnie and Marie. Moose was a little bit country, I was a little bit rock 'n' roll but in the end we were both part of the family.

When we were finally left alone during the day, we got to know each other better.

It turned out Moose was from the same shelter I was from. When I found this out, a flurry of questions came to mind.

Had she encountered Ratchet? Yes she had, and she was a mean caretaker.

Was Candyman still running the joint? No he had been adopted out.

Were dogs still coming in with balls and leaving without them? Yes, and the scandal didn't stop there. Cats were victims, too!

On and on it went until my curiosity had been quenched.

After we had talked ourselves out, our relationship turned into a physical one. No not that kind of physical, but physical as in running, playing, chasing.

I lay in the family room, minding my own business and chewing a sneaker. It was a Nike if I recall. It wasn't bad, but a true connoisseur knows Reeboks taste the best.

Moose strutted up to me and purred contently, pressing her furry head against my face before taking off in a sprint. This was the equivalent of her meowing, "Nananana! You can't catch me"—a challenge any self-respecting canine cannot turn down.

I pursued her out of the room and down the hall, my eyes focused on her tail. Just as I was about to put my mouth around it, she took a hard left, a move I wasn't ready for. I slid forward, right into the wall. Bam . . . I looked up, thankful the picture over my head didn't fall.

Moose stood at the top of the stairs, mocking me. I regained my composure and lunged toward her. She took off again. It was now clear that she was toying with me. Oh, this one was a player, she was.

I chased her onto a windowsill, where I barked wildly until she admitted defeat.

It was a game we played often. When we weren't running around, we loved watching TV together. My parents often left it on to keep us from being lonely. It really works. I lay down in the sunny part of the room and Moose snuggles up against me. People call it spooning. I call it ladling.

More often than not, we drift in and out of sleep to the likes of *The Price Is Right*, *Love Connection*, and *One Life to Live*. As a bonus, if anyone ever needs a lawyer for an accident claim, we can give them the phone numbers of at least ten questionable firms.

I was surprised by how quickly our bond grew. Maybe it was because cats seemed to be more trustworthy than humans. Well, Moose was anyway. We had a great relationship.

The bond between Moose and my parents wasn't going nearly as well.

"Moose! Get down!" was the second most heard phrase in the house. The most heard phrase was, "Bo, NO!"

Moose had a habit of jumping up on the counters and sampling whatever food was up there. She also crapped in the house. Granted it was in a box dedicated to the task, but someone still had to clean it.

I told Moose to give it time, they'd come around.

Weeks after Moose came home, my mother stopped going to work. Word was that she didn't really like her job, and she didn't appreciate the boss's attitude. That was fine by me; now there were three of us to hang out all day. But I was soon to learn that life is neither fair nor kind.

I awoke one morning, after having slept in with my father, and noticed that something in the house felt different. I nudged the old man to get up and let me out to pee, which he did.

When I came back in, I still couldn't shake the feeling that something wasn't quite right. I went looking for Moose—I had a kink in my neck from my soft pillow and could use one of those body kneadings she was famous for. I looked downstairs. Not there. I searched upstairs. Not there, either. Hmmm . . . where was she hiding?

I searched again and again, growing more frantic with every passing moment, only to realize she was not at home. She was gone!

Where was she? Had she gone to visit some friends in the country? Or did she follow her lifelong dream of going to the Big Apple and trying out for *Cats*? Or was it more ominous than that? Maybe she was on the streets of the inner city, forced to sell her body to dirty, old tomcats just to get enough food to survive?

Days went by, then weeks. My good friend had vanished like a plate of unattended cookies on the living room table. Even the rides with my mother didn't pack the same punch, now that I knew I'd be coming home to a deserted house.

I felt lonely, and empty.

Even my father noticed the change. After coming home late one night, he glanced down at me and said, "What's the problem, buddy?"

I turned to him and asked, "What's happened to Moose? Is she suffering alone out there?"

He didn't answer, but did what he always did under difficult circumstances. He loaded me up with a handful of treats. Not a bad tactic under normal circumstances, but these were extraordinary times. I couldn't be cheered up. The not knowing was eating me alive.

Then, one night, I overheard my parents talking.

"So how's Moose doing?" my father asked as he finished off one of my mother's dinner specialties.

"Well, Marcy says she's still adjusting to living with all the other cats in her house."

"Adjusting? That sounds like she's not doing that great, then."

"She'll be all right; Marcy loves cats. Besides, didn't you notice there's no cat hair on your spoon anymore? It's amazing what happens when you no longer have a cat crawling around in the utensil drawer."

"I just hope we didn't make a mistake giving her away," my father said in a worried voice, "but then again, you seem much more rested now that Moose isn't jumping on your chest to wake you up every night."

"I didn't mind that, but I just couldn't take her jumping on the counters anymore. And when she licked that nice chicken I cooked for you, I just lost it."

I could see her replay the chicken-licking incident in her mind over and over as she spoke. "Do you want some more dinner?"

"If you don't mind making more."

"It's no bother. Do you want chicken or beef?"

"Does it really matter? It's Oodles of Noodles."

So there it was. Moose hadn't left of her own free will at all, but was given away to the very same Marcy who had helped to pick her out!

I shuddered at the thought of Moose as the latest jewel in Marcy Catcollector's crown. You see, as legend goes, Marcy Catcollector had actually taught her cats to fetch a crumpled up piece of paper and then return it to her: homegrown calico retrievers, if you will. No doubt there was torture involved to get felines to do this because, no offense to the cats reading this, they aren't too bright.

Now my beloved friend was in her clutches. What daily horror was Moose facing? What torture was being inflicted on my lounge buddy? Why did Marcy need my companion? My Moose?!

What could I do? I got all shook up, I threw down my gun, he called me a pa, I called him a son. Wait, *wait*! That's a Johnny Cash song and there's not even a character named Sue in this story. Do you know why I love the man in black? That's right, because he tastes like chicken. Sorry, sometimes my ADD gets in the way. Anyway, back to the story.

Since my communication skills were limited, I was forced to share my misgivings in a most natural way.

I started to pee in the house.

On the surface, we went about our morning routines. After my father left for work, my mother took me for my walk. I made a great show of peeing on telephone poles and fire hydrants, but unbeknownst to my mother, I started keeping a little juice in reserve to use at my discretion, if you know what I mean.

Once we returned home, I'd wait until my mother was in another room before seeking out an item at eye level, or below, and dousing it with a healthy splash of Eau De Bo cologne. Targets varied from the VCR to the couch and to my favorite . . . the TV.

My mother was upset. She was used to living in an odor-free home, and even I had to admit, it wasn't easy enjoying *Oprah* with an electric-charged urine smell coming from the boob tube.

"Maybe he's got a bladder infection?" my father suggested.

"I don't have a bladder infection! I miss Moose! Bring her back and we all go back to the way things were."

"Bo, be quiet," my mother scolded, then she picked up the phone and made two appointments: one with the carpet cleaners and one with the vet.

It wasn't long before I was back in the cold exam room. The doctor felt and prodded along my private area, acting as if he were the second coming of James Herriot. He took some blood along with a little bit of pride and told me to go into the bathroom and pee in a cup. When I was done I put my name on it and placed it in the medicine cabinet with two-way doors.

Do you know how hard that is to do with the oversized, furry paws I possess? Peeing took me forever and getting it into the small cup was no easy task. It turned out that writing my name on the container was the easy part.

When it was over, my mother drove me home, but not before stopping at the local ice cream stand to get me a baby cone. Even when she wasn't happy with me, she always thought of me. I would probably have gotten a banana split if I had been pooping uncontrollably in the house rather than merely peeing.

A few days later the clinic called and confirmed that I did not have a bladder infection, but a bad attitude. Of course I had a bad attitude! I ask you, did Mrs. Hoffa have a bad attitude after Jimmy disappeared? I'll guarantee you she did, although I'll concede that she probably didn't wee on her TV.

Afterward, my parents discussed my "issue" at length.

"You think he's mad because we changed his food?"

"No. He likes variety. You think it's because we move around in bed too much?"

"No. He sleeps right through it. Maybe it's because he's only escaping twice a week now."

"No. He breaks free whenever he wants. Maybe it's because . . ."

Oh boy . . . this could take forever. If I could have meowed, I would have.

Seven theories later they came upon the motivation for my inappropriate behavior. They called Marcy Catcollector, thus securing Moose's release.

We all make mistakes, and they were open to correcting theirs, so the least I could do was let them off the hook. I decided to stop making lemonade on their things.

Moose and I were together again. We caught up on our soaps, snuggled in the sunlit living room, and enjoyed each

Vanity Plates I'd Get

(If I Could Get Insurance and Own a Car)

other's company. Our relationship was stronger and better than before.

My relationship with my parents, however, had suffered. They needed to regain my trust after what they'd done.

They'd have plenty of opportunities, especially around dinnertime.

CHAPTER 6

The Hand That Rocked the Cradle

On a small, quiet side street peppered with sensible homes, a car teeter-totters atop a four-foot-high retaining wall, its two occupants sitting in the eerie silence of an adrenaline aftermath. In the driver's seat is my mother; occupying the suicide seat is an adorable fuzzy-faced canine: me.

The night had started out promising . . . how could it have gone so horribly wrong?

I blame it on Fahrvergnügen.

Fahrvergnügen. "What is it?" you ask. It's basically when humans become one with their car. Some people have it, others don't. My mother, she didn't have it.

Due to her parents' aptly placed fear in her driving skills, my mother didn't learn to drive until she was twenty-one years old—old enough to vote, old enough to drink, and too old to date Hugh Hefner. Perhaps due to being a late bloomer, she never gained adequate confidence behind the wheel, which resulted in numerous mishaps throughout the course of her life.

On that wintry eve, less than a year after my adoption, my mother decided to head over to her parents' house for a free meal and some conversation. I was lucky enough to be asked along for the ride and hopefully for some treats. I zipped up my fur suit and hopped into my mother's Ford Mustang, a vehicle that—at best—handled poorly in the winter and that had recently had issues with its gear shifter mysteriously popping into drive. Based on my experiences, it wasn't so much a mystery as it was driver error, but who am I to judge? I don't have opposable thumbs.

I jumped up onto the cold front seat. Seconds later, my ears flapped in the gusts of frigid upstate New York air coming from the vehicle's vents. A few blocks from our destination I picked up on the scent of my grandfather's meal. My drool started its uncontrollable flow; my grandparents had proven themselves to be the easiest treat targets this side of the Hudson River. A few hearty sniffs confirmed I would be partaking in some of their brisket, decked out in their famous homemade sauce.

As we turned left onto my grandparents' dead-end road, our headlights illuminated several trash cans placed at the ends of the driveways. Garbage night. Yum. My mother slowed down a few houses from our destination and peered through the frosty passenger window before coming to a complete halt. "Bo, what is that on the side of the road? Is that a doll cradle? Now, why would somebody throw that away?"

Why she found it necessary to ask me questions when I had food on my mind always perplexed me, so I ignored her. As she was apt to do she answered her own question, "I don't know why anyone would toss that out, but I bet Aunt Marcy would love it."

She laid out the strategy. "Here's the deal, Bo. I'm going to drive around again so the cradle is on my side of the car. I'll stop, grab it, and drive off without anyone being the wiser."

I wanted to reply, "Hey, I'm not on a scavenger hunt, I

just want dinner," but I knew that once my mother got a thought in her head there was no stopping her.

She drove to the end of the street, turned around, and headed back for her prize. As we neared the crib, she swerved to the other side of the street so she could reach it from her side. She put her foot on the brake and shifted the car into neutral, then stopped in a spot where she could get it and make a quick getaway. Or so she thought.

When she opened the car door the cradle was enticingly close but still a bridge too far. My mother was forced to lean way, way out of the car in a very unstable position; her body halfway out of the car with her left hand on the cold road for support as she reached for the cradle with the right. Her tiny foot was barely in contact with the brake pedal. It was clear she needed help, my help, to get her reward.

My mind raced for a solution, the only reasonable of which was to fetch the cradle for her. Heck, it's the least I could do for the meal that awaited me. Besides, I'm not easily embarrassed about picking garbage. In fact, I rather enjoy the notoriety of it.

As my mother leaned toward the door, I leaped over her to lend a helping paw. In midflight, my legs hit the gearshift, and I tumbled, rather ungracefully, into my mother.

It was like my mother was a cue ball and I a cue stick. I should have called the shot: "Mommie Dearest, street corner pocket," because as soon as I bumped into her, she rolled out of the car and right onto the road.

I scrambled to steady myself only to find I was now sitting in the driver seat!

I looked down through the open doorway of the car, and there lay my mother facedown on the cold asphalt. That must suck for her, I thought, until I realized the car was moving! Now it sucked *for me* because I was going for a ride, whether I liked it or not.

The car was steadily gaining speed when I glanced into my rearview mirror to see my mother frantically scramble to her feet, only to slip on a small patch of ice a few short steps later. She'd never make it in time. I was on my own, driving without a license.

Well, without a driver's license that is. I had a dog license.

I began to appreciate the difficulty in controlling a car. The concept wasn't difficult to understand; position paws at 10 and 2 on the steering wheel, aim high in steering, and swerve at all squirrels you see. But it's just that with my fuzzy mitts I couldn't get a grip on the steering wheel plus my legs were too short to reach the brake pedal. I was helpless, and danger quickly approached. I hurtled toward a shiny new Cadillac with frightening speed; one last glance in my rearview mirror showed my mother pulling herself up and sprinting in my direction. A surreal feeling enveloped me and everything moved in slow motion. I could see my mother opening her mouth, yelling "Baaaaaaaaaaaaa Ohhhhhhhhhhhhhh! Staaaaaahhhhhppppp Thaaaaaa Kaaaaaaahhhrr!" Her arms and legs pumped up and down, but she still seemed so far away. I was now so close to the Cadillac I could breathe in that new car smell.

I had a moment to wonder if this was the end of Bo Hoefinger—certified genius, uncertified driver. I knew I should have buckled up.

Not only is it a good idea, it's the law.

I braced myself for the crash when a hand reached into the car and grasped the steering wheel. It was my mother! In a move worthy of a Hollywood stuntman, she jerked the wheel of the old Mustang, pulled herself into the car on top of me, and swerved out of the way of the parked car just in time.

Huh—maybe she'd learned something in driving school after all.

Unfortunately, we were now headed directly toward a four-foot-high retaining wall. And this time, my mother was too slow to react.

The snow at the base of the retaining wall was like an aerial ski ramp. When we hit it, the car jerked skyward, but instead of getting airborne and doing a whirly bird at the top, we lurched to a stop.

As we sat in silence, I knew my mother was thinking, Oh please God, if you could show me just a little bit of mercy and not let anyone see what happened I'll be forever grateful.

I remember what I was thinking: I hope the brisket doesn't dry out.

It wasn't until we climbed down from the car that we realized it was wedged on top of the wooden wall, with the front end over a snow-covered lawn and the back end hanging over the road.

The porch lights of the home turned on and the front door opened, revealing a man in a nighttime robe and slippers.

"What are you doing? Why is your car on top of my wall?" he screamed.

"I . . . I don't know!" my mother responded in despair. "I . . . I must have hit some black ice and spun out of control."

"I don't see any black ice out here."

"That's why they call it black ice. You can't see it."

The man rolled his eyes, then took a good look at my mother, vague recognition dawning on his face. "Hey, aren't you Gordon and Barbara's daughter?"

Sheepishly my mother replied in the affirmative, looking like a schoolgirl who had just been caught smoking in the girls' room.

"Can I borrow your phone? I really need to call Triple A," she asked.

"We can call your parents if you like?"

"No that's okay. I'd rather just call Triple A."

"Sure I understand." Then, trying to make small talk he said, "So, I heard you're married."

"Yes, but before you go there, I don't want to call him, either."

I understood her hesitancy. After all, she was a garbage picker who fell out of her car. I tried to hide behind her legs, lest I be recognized as well. It's not easy being part of this family; humiliation comes with the territory.

When the tow truck arrived, I overheard the driver saying into his radio, "I don't know how she got there; all I'm telling you is that her car is stuck on top of a wall. Yeah, on top . . . about four feet high. No, I don't have my camera with me."

Once the car was back on solid ground with no major harm done, my mother decided to forgo dinner with her parents. She gave me an apologetic pat on the head and told me she needed a night to sleep on it, to digest the evening's events.

The only thing I'd digest that night would be some dry kibble from home.

When my mother finally worked up the nerve to tell her sister the story, all her sister said was, "So, where's the crib?"

Doggienügen. "What is it?" you ask. It's basically when dog becomes one with their family. Some dogs have it, others don't. I didn't have it, yet.

But I would.

CHAPTER 7

This Old House

"Oh crap, I'm late!"

The declaration startled me out of my sleep. It was a Saturday morning and that meant only one thing: my father was late for his tee time again.

He was already scurrying about the room looking for a clean shirt, clean shorts, and clean socks to put on by the time I lifted my head. My nose confirmed his dirty underwear was good to go, complete with racing stripe down the middle.

After finding a wrinkly shirt and a pair of not so flattering shorts, he grabbed a hat to cover his poofy hair. Judge Smails may have thought he looked good, but to the rest of the world he looked ridiculous.

I pleaded with my mother to wake up and save the family name. All she mustered up was a weak, "Make sure to let Bo out to pee."

Moments later, as was routine, the retractable leash was secured to my collar and I was let out to do my business.

I spotted a periwinkle and doused it with a vengeance. Ahhh, that felt good.

After two shakes (three and they'll accuse you of playing with it) I felt the tug of the leash, and just like that, my bathroom break was over. I walked through the door and glanced up at him. I gave it one last shot.

"Don't do it, man. Have some self-respect and change the outfit."

But he didn't listen. He just threw me half the granola bar he was eating before hurrying out of the house.

I lay down and chewed on the honey oat goodness that was my treat. In the distance the garage door opened, the car roared to life, and the familiar sound of the family automobile signaled another day alone with my mother.

That is, until a thunderous noise, like the sound of a stick of dynamite going off, erupted from the garage.

It was so loud, I nearly pooped my fur suit.

My mother heard it, too, and came running down the stairs. I caught a glimpse of the garage as she opened the door. My father was nowhere to be seen, but the garage floor was now covered in a lovely white, eggshell finish. Closer inspection revealed the old man had backed over a gallon container of paint, causing it to explode. In his hurry to get to the course, he didn't even bother to stop and check out the damage.

With focus like that you'd think he'd be better than a 105 golfer.

Although my mother didn't understand his actions, I did. He simply had something better to do.

I can't explain how I knew, especially since, at first sniff, my father and I had little in common. Objectively speaking: he's a provider, I'm a providee; he's book smart, I'm street smart; he's introverted, I'm extroverted; he chews his peanuts, I lick mine. It could be said he's the yin to my yang, the meow to my woof, the Bo No! to my oh Yes!

But experiences like the "One Minute Garage Makeover" at least hinted at the fact we had some things in common.

I couldn't have come up with a better reply than the one he used after returning from golf that day.

"Paint? What are you talking about? I didn't drive over anything."

Deny, deny, deny.

There was hope for him after all, and a closer look revealed we were alike in many ways.

When it comes to most things he is indifferent, aloof, and oblivious to the world around him. The same has been said about me. Mention golf, computers, or beer to him, or walk, ride, or chipmunk to me and suddenly we're like a strung-out kitty ready to do anything for a fix of catnip.

My mother knew this, too. That's why I had a leash and my father had a honey-do list longer than a dachshund.

So when my father showed the smallest interest in starting a home project she made sure to take advantage. Mind you, my father's handyman prowess was somewhere between a six-year-old girl playing with her Easy Bake Oven and a seven-year-old boy playing with a wad of Play-Doh. Regardless, she showed faith in him, more faith than I ever received.

Earlier in the year, when one of the faucets needed replacing in the downstairs bathroom, he attacked it like Bob Vila. Except he forgot to turn off the valve that controls the water flow to the sink. I don't mean to imply he overlooked that detail, he just didn't know enough to do it. Nine hundred gallons of water later, he found the main shut-off valve.

And then there was the beautiful decorative molding he installed over our front door, to add a little "class" to the outside of the house. To this day it hangs upside down, just like the day he installed it. Classy guy, that father of mine.

Of course I'd be remiss not to mention the time he decided to install cable TV in one of the guest bedrooms. He climbed into the attic to lay the cable, and moments later, his leg crashed through the bedroom ceiling. Sadly, he was surprised to learn Sheetrock wouldn't hold a 180-plus pound man.

His tainted repair history didn't stop my mother from trying again. But she figured this latest project was different— a joint effort by my parents—that consisted of converting an upstairs bedroom into an office. This particular job wasn't so much a "conversion" as it was a new paint job and the switching out of a bed for a desk. Even my father couldn't screw that up.

Project Day arrived, and my parents got to work. As the designated superintendent of the job, I alternately snoozed and supervised from a safe vantage point in the hallway. My father was responsible for painting the walls a deep burgundy, just like the coloring of the fine wine I enjoy. My mother was in charge of the trim, including fresh coats of white paint on the windows.

When my mother finished up her first coat, she put the pan of paint on the floor. Inspecting my father's work, she said, "There are so many small holes. We need some spackle and sandpaper to make this look right. I'm going to run to the hardware store."

Trying to get out of his work, my father offered, "No, I'll go. You can stay."

"No, you need to finish the first coat on these walls and start on the second. I'll only be a few minutes," she countered before adding, "Oh, if you leave this room, make sure to close the door. I don't want Moose to come in and jump up on the wet windowsill."

"Okay."

"Did you hear me? Make sure the door is closed."

"I heard you. I'll make sure to close the door if I leave."

With that, my mother gave me a pat on the head and left the house.

Predictably, a few moments later my father lost his passion for painting. He put down his paint roller and headed out of the room. Where he was going, I'm not sure, but I could tell by his body language that the last thing he was thinking about was closing that door.

As the superintendent, I felt it was my responsibility to get him back on the right track. I got up from my position in the hallway and blocked his way. I looked up at him, then at the door, back up at him, and to the door again. He just said, "C'mon, buddy, let's get some lunch."

Lunch? Let's go!

Down the stairs and to the kitchen we went. I had the bologna; he had the ham.

Meanwhile, Moose took this opportunity to slink her way into the new office. I've known a lot of cats in my day, and I don't think any of them could resist an open door, a wet pan of paint, and a just painted windowsill. To Moose, it was an open invitation. She confided in me later that if they didn't want her in there, they should have put up a wet paint sign. But they didn't.

Moose explored the room for the best cat-nap location, ultimately deciding on the open window. She lay down on the sill, stretching herself across the entire window. What luck! What a view!

And the wet paint had the added benefit of cooling her fur.

She drifted off to sleep with a warm spring breeze blowing in her face.

After lunch, my father and I headed back to work. With a "this sucks" sigh, he walked into the room, grabbed his roller, and started to paint, unaware of Moose's presence.

I watched in anticipation from my post in the hallway.

How long would it take him to realize that she was sleeping on the wet windowsill? Would Moose wake up in time? Would she escape? If caught, how would she be cleaned? Would she get spanked? Put in time-out? Sent back to the cat pound?

It was high drama, and I have to admit, better than an episode of *COPS*. Bad girl, bad girl . . . watchya gonna do, watchya gonna do when he comes at you?!

My answer came in less than a second. "What the . . . Moose! Get off of there!"

Moose didn't budge. She was never one to take kindly to verbal direction, and certainly not from the old man. It was an attitude I reinforced with her often, and it was good to see it in action. I beamed with pride.

My father burned with anger. He lunged at her, giving Moose the motivation she needed to jump. She leaped from the windowsill to the floor . . . and directly into the pan full of white paint. The startled look on Moose's face indicated she had not planned on landing there. The look was priceless, accentuated by her half-white face.

I wished I had popcorn.

"No! Get over here!" he screamed.

All the players in this comedy knew Moose must not get out of the room. My father made one last swipe. He was slow, the cat quick. It was like watching Andre the Giant trying to catch a chicken. A second later, she was past him, past me in the hallway, and down the stairs.

"Moose, get back here!" he yelled as he stumbled over me, nearly falling down the stairs.

The telltale signs of her escape were quite evident by the white paw prints she left with each step. Let's just say she didn't take the road less traveled. She made her way down the red-carpeted steps, over the oriental rug, and into the newly carpeted family room; each step leaving a bit of her legacy behind.

She later told me that her goal was to hide, but that when she saw the paw prints she left behind, she knew that was out of the question. Her objective changed to running all over the house and confusing my father with all the different paw tracks before finding a resting spot. Not a bad plan considering the old man had difficulty finding the end of his own driveway sometimes.

I sat in the living room with a great vantage point on the action. My father was always one step behind Moose. Every time he got close enough, she'd outmaneuver him and continue onward. Moose's plan was working until she took an ill-conceived left turn into the bathroom. I heard some banging, some swearing, and a loud meow. My father had finally caught her and promptly sent her to the Gulag, otherwise known as the cellar.

Silence settled over the house, and everything seemed perfectly normal, save for my father's occasional muttered profanities and little white paw prints all over the house. If we were a hospital it would have been acceptable. I can hear the receptionist say, "Yes sir, just follow the white paw prints and they'll take you directly to X-Ray."

But this wasn't a hospital.

Operation Pawprints was deployed and time was of the essence. If my mother saw this she would freak out. I'm serious; she would *freak out*! My father grabbed rolls of paper towels, warm water, and dish soap and scoured the hardwood floors. He then moved on to the carpeted areas, cleaning with gazelle-like speed.

All was cleaned up by the time my bark announced my mother's return. My father ran upstairs to make believe he was working on the room, and I sat waiting for the door to open. It was as if nothing had happened at all.

My Favorite Movies/Shows

Old Yeller Did you know he didn't really yell a lot, just got a bad rap early in his career and was never able to shake it?

Reservoir Dogs Not about sporting dogs but just as violent.

Westminster Kennel Show Hoowah! Who doesn't like to look at the ladies when they're all dolled up?

Scarface "Say hello to my little friend, Snoopy."

The Shaggy DA Not sure if a dog being a lawyer is a good or bad thing for us.

Teen Wolf That dog could play some serious round ball although the interspecies dating thing creeps me out a bit.

Cujo Cujo running into the car door—one of the best scenes ever in cinematic history; I wonder who the stunt dog was.

The Godfather Thank goodness it wasn't a dog's head in the bed.

Doggie Howser Young dog makes it big in medicine.

Dog Day Afternoon Dog day afternoons are made to hold up banks? C'mon, Hollywood, stop with the stereotypes.

Bo and his agent

"How's my little BoBo?" she asked as she walked through the door.

After the standard pat of the head and the stroke of the chest, she made a beeline to check on the status of the upstairs project.

She gave my father a confused look, for there hadn't been a lot of progress since she left.

"I didn't get much done. I was looking for the spackle to fix the dart holes. Do you know where it is?"

"I told you, that's what I went to the store for."

"Oh. I guess that's why I couldn't find it."

Quick . . . and devious. I like it.

And just like that, it seemed the end of it. That is until two minutes later.

"Hey, what happened to the carpet? It's got paint all over it! And the stairs, they have paint all over them, too. What the heck happened here?"

"What are you talking about? I don't see anything."

"Of course you don't, you're a man."

Then, with the verbal equivalent of grabbing him by the ear and sticking his nose in it, she yelled, "Look. Right there. There's white paint on the carpet . . . and it goes all the way up the stairs . . . and over here in the living room . . . and there in the dining room . . . and there . . ." and on and on it went.

Regrettably for him he cleans like he listens, not very well.

It wasn't long before my mother had a full confession spilling from his lips.

I sat at his feet, looking up at him and shaking my head. He broke the Golden Rule: never, ever admit to your crime. It was clear he'd need more coaching from me.

He received "the look" from my mother followed by a

verbal reprimand. "I told you to close the door! You're as bad as Bo. You two never listen to a thing I say!"

Welcome to the club.

If he kept up this pace, it wouldn't be long before he grew a tail.

CHAPTER 8

The Shot Heard Round the World

I love sleep. I love my parents' bed. I love to sleep in my parents' bed.

Because of this, you might remember that one of the first things I did after moving in was to make sure I was allowed to come up on their nightly resting place. It's a simple process when you're, how should I put this . . . 100 percent snugglable. It doesn't hurt if your parents are looking to share their abundance of love, too.

Every evening I jump up, put my head on one of their chests, and just stare at them. Every once in a while, I lift my head and nudge a hand to keep the affection flowing. Before long, they drift off to sleep and I wedge myself between the two of them. It is as simple as that to get a lifetime membership to their bed.

The best part is I don't have to pay an annual renewal fee.

But there is one rule that cannot be broken. If I'm dirty, I'm relegated to the floor. No, not as in dirty curse words, but rather dirty fur. Although I'm a meticulous groomer, there are times I get a little "gamey," especially if I've forsaken the shower for a month or two. More often than not, an escape leads to such a cleansing.

As you'd expect, I scheduled my escapes accordingly, and followed a most effective plan.

I'd wait for my father to become immersed in an outdoors project, which he usually did with the garage door up. Then I'd wait for my mother to open the door leading to the garage and call out to see if he wanted lunch. This was my opportunity. Before she even had a chance to register what was happening, I'd squeeze between her legs and bust through the opening.

Even though my risk of capture was high at this point, I always paused, taking in the scene.

I'd look at my father, and then at the wide expanse of openness beyond the door.

He'd look at me, and then at the wide expanse of openness beyond the door.

We both calculated in our heads the chance of my escape based upon our proximity to each other.

Regardless of his high math score on the SATs, my father was no match for my wit. If the odds were in my favor, I'd be off in a sprint, through the door and to the vast wilderness before he even finished filling in his name with a number 2 pencil. If the odds were poor, I'd wag my tail and walk to him for a nice head scratch. I was such a good boy. Oh, yes I was.

If I made my way to freedom, I'd often head to the creek a few hundred yards behind the house. It was a deliciously muddy, cool, and refreshing stream even in the summer. After chasing the local wildlife I'd finish off the day with a dip. And since this was *my* backyard I needn't worry about anyone steeling my fur suit from the river bank.

I'd return from my wanderings smelling like Wet Dog by

Giorgi Armani. My father would thrust me into the bathtub for a good scrubbing before allowing me back in bed at night. I guess he preferred Old Spice.

Of course I put up a fight as my father tried to put me in the tub, but it was all for show. I mean, c'mon, what part of getting a warm bath along with a deep rubdown is not to like? Even so, my favorite part was shaking my fur out and covering my half-soaked father with even more water.

I guess the only real downside to my frequent escapes was that it led my parents to ensure I got my annual shots. These shots, coupled with heartworm pills and the flea and tick solutions, made sure I wasn't giving my parents an unwanted gift.

Other than a bad attitude, that is.

Payback day arrived, and I was shuffled off to the vet, where I was sure I'd be told to open my snout and say "Wooooooooooooooof," turn my head and cough, and to hold still as I'm jabbed with a needle.

My father kindly agreed to take me—an oddity because as it was a Saturday, one of his only days off. Although it was a nice gesture, I was a little worried, as my father isn't as thorough about my health care as my mother.

"I'm taking Bo to the vet now. Is there anything I need to know?" he yelled.

"Make sure to ask them about his anal glands."

"His anal glands?"

"Honey, he's been scooting across the floor a lot and he keeps licking his butt."

"Can you just write that down on a piece of paper? I'd rather just slip them a note than have to use the word *anal* in public."

"Just ask them. They'll know what you mean."

Reluctantly my father agreed. "Okay, I will."

He and I both knew he was lying.

I jumped into the passenger seat, ready to go. I wasn't looking forward to seeing the doctor, but one thing I had learned with this family, life is all about the journey; it didn't matter if the final destination was heaven or hell. It was a warm spring day and, not to brag, the green of the new foliage brought out the color in my eyes. Flower, a collie I dated once, told me that. We broke up because she was pasty white and smelled funny.

You know who else was pasty white and smelled funny? My veterinarian. But that's a relationship I couldn't get out of without a permission slip from my parents, and I certainly wasn't getting one on this trip.

It was a joyous ride through the neighborhoods of our small city. I smashed my face against the window to get a better look at the flowers sporting their new colors, the endless smattering of strip malls, and the church adjacent to the local PetSmart; the day's message on the sign was thought provoking, as always: "Dog who fart in church, sit in own pew," or maybe it was "Dog spelled backwards is God." Regardless, both were original and inspirational.

To a dog, the area around the vet's office was akin to a mailbox after a two-week vacation: totally stuffed. There were many messages to be checked, and it was going to take a long time to go through them all and reply.

"C'mon, Bo. Make it quick," my father insisted.

Ha! Fat chance, I thought as I sniffed my way through the mail.

"What? Huckleberry was not a purebred?" Oh my, his reputation is ruined!

"Harley has a drinking problem?" Well that's not a shocker if you ever saw how much water ended up on the floor after a typical binge. I hope rehab helps him.

"Riley called Pumpkin a bitch." I don't like that kind of language, but truth be told she did have pups last year.

And scrawled on the fire hydrant was *"For a good time bark up Piper at woof, woof, woof."*

"Woof, woof, woof." Darn, no answer.

And on and on it went.

Finally, a really strong tug hurtled me forward onto the paved walkway, through an open door, and into the waiting room.

Once checked in, we sat down and waited for our turn. We waited and waited. After that, we waited some more. If wait times were any indication of the quality of veterinary care received, I was about to get the best dog treatment ever.

My father perused *Dog Fancy*, but I wasn't about to just sit there like a cat, or a trained dog. I seized the opportunity to secure my position as king of the vet clinic by smelling the other "patients" in the room, scoping out the dog biscuit container on the counter, and throwing dirty looks at the cage of kittens in the corner.

With my father's attention diverted elsewhere it was time to mark my territory in the waiting room. Dogs who pee without raising their leg always think theirs is the best way. To the contrary, not only does raising your leg boost pee pressure, but with a quick turn of the hips you can increase your coverage area twofold! Up went my leg, but not too high, and I peed what I had left in my emergency tank. I was finished by the time I heard my name yelled in vain.

"Bo, *stop!* Bad boy! Bo is a bad boy! A bad boy!" It was my father. The others in the room shook their heads with displeasure, wondering why this man couldn't control his dog and thanking God I wasn't theirs.

I gave my father a look that said, "Who's *your* daddy?!" He shot back a nasty look and gave me a quick yank of the leash to show me who was boss. Who was he kidding?

I lay down, put my head on my paws, and contently

watched a pimple-laden, brace-faced kid earning minimum wage clean up my mess.

I was king of this castle.

Our name was called shortly thereafter and we proceeded to a second waiting room. After some time the door opened and one of the technicians entered. He was a young tech who couldn't have been more than twenty-one. I had never seen him before and I wondered if he was even licensed.

"I see Bo is in here for his checkup and annual shots."

"Yes."

"How's everything been with him? Is there anything I need to be aware of?"

"He's a little stubborn, but other than that he's been great." After the nipple incident, he was gun-shy about asking any of my mother's questions, especially the ones that needed a note. But we already knew my anal glands would have to wait for the next visit.

After a cursory review of my body, the technician pulled a medicine-filled needle from the cabinet. He squatted down in front of me while showering me with words of praise for being such a good boy. Two things immediately popped into my head: (1) nobody ever tells me I'm a good boy unless something bad is about to happen, and (2) this guy had a needle in his hand. My spidey sense tingled.

As he bent down in front of me, I started to back away. Unfortunately my father squatted down behind me and held me between his legs to the point where I couldn't back up any farther. This position allowed him to control me from behind, described as a rear mount in wrestling circles. Not Jimmy "Superfly" Snuka wrestling, but real college-style wrestling.

The needle flashed in the fluorescent lights as he angled it toward my left shoulder, looking for a good fleshy area to puncture my skin. As he grabbed my fur I made sure not to squirm. I had a plan and it would require impeccable timing to pull it off. I waited as patiently as an owner reading *Dog Fancy* magazine in a waiting room. Yeah, that patiently.

When the needle touched my fur, I sprang to life by twisting my upper body out of the needle's intended path.

The technician, Mr. Professional, missed me. Dog wins; technician loses.

But the real loser was my father, for even though the technician hadn't injected me, he somehow managed to pierce my father just above his left knee.

"Oww! Whaddya doing?" cried my father, a trickle of blood flowing down his leg. That will teach him not to wear shorts when bringing me to the vet.

"Did I get you?"

"Yeah, you got me! I can't believe it. You just gave me a shot."

"Oh, my God! I am so sorry!"

"Oh, man, that stings. That was a clean needle wasn't it? I'm not going to get AIDS or anything crazy like that am I?"

He was on the verge of flipping out.

"You should be okay."

"Should be or will be?"

"Will be."

"Are you sure nothing is going to happen to me? There isn't any crazy dog diseases going around that I can catch, are there?"

"No, the needle was sterilized. I barely shot any of the actual vaccine into your leg. You'll be fine."

That calmed my father down.

"Oh, man. Do you have a napkin so I can wipe the blood off my leg?"

"Sure, here ya go. I'm real sorry about this."

"Have you ever shot anybody else before? Is your nickname Sniper around here?"

The technician stood awkwardly by while my father finished wiping his leg.

I stood by, too, but not awkwardly. Unless by awkwardly you mean laying there with your paw over your stomach because it hurt so much from laughing.

"I'm really sorry about this," the technician said again, and then hesitantly continued, "I'm almost too embarrassed to ask this, but can you hold Bo again so I can give him his shot?"

"All right, but make sure you get him this time!"

"I will."

I couldn't believe it! He was going to trust this guy to do this again? Well, at least he wasn't trying to inoculate my anal glands.

My father got behind me and held me tight. There was no getting out of the way this time and I took it like a dog. Sure it hurt, but it didn't stop me from laughing on the inside.

As the technician left the room, my father said to him, "You really need to be more careful."

"I will be," he assured my father. Then trying to lighten the mood he finished with, "And don't worry, I'll only charge you for Bo's shot."

Every bad experience has a silver lining and this one was no different. After the shot my father received, he never had to worry about getting rabies.

But I would soon find out, some trips to the veterinary facility were no laughing matter.

CHAPTER 9

Mini or Maxi

"**Just hold on,** little buddy. We're almost there!" my father screamed in a panicky voice over the wail of the ambulance siren. I could barely make out his huge head hovering over me. The worry in his words served as a sharp contrast to the feeling of peace slowly coming over me. I fought to remain conscious but struggled to keep my eyes from rolling into the back of my head.

"Whatever you do, don't go through the light. Stay with me, buddy."

I lay in the fetal position, my head in my mother's lap, as we sped toward the local pet hospital. I had learned to love my life, my family, my treats. Was all my hard work for naught?

When we arrived at the clinic, the vet and his assistant rushed to the ambulance and carried me inside. They transferred me onto the cold surface of the operating table and hooked me up to an IV. Once the anesthesia kicked in, the pain subsided and I floated above my body, taking in the panic of the room below. The scene was eerily distant. As distant as the calming bright light above me was comfortably close.

I was straddling two worlds. On the one side a bright light shone. It smelled of roast beef—freshly roasted beef au jus to be exact. On the other side, a gray light glimmered. It smelled of salami—my father's salami breath to be exact. The chasm between the two was growing. I needed to make a decision, and fast.

Would I choose to come back to my life of old or move on to a bright future?

I weighed my alternatives and decided on my answer. It was easy, I would choose . . .

Cut! Stop right there!

Maybe, just maybe, I'm embellishing the events that transpired that particular weekend. Sure I had a near-death experience, but that's no excuse to make the story grander than it really was. I'm not human, after all. And besides I don't want a *Million Little Pieces* type of controversy hanging over my head

So, before I go further please note that I never took an ambulance to the animal hospital, I never had to choose between two worlds, and if I ever smelled my father's salami breath up close, I wouldn't be alive to type this today.

Although I may have been pushing the exaggeration-o-meter to the dial labeled 11, in no way does that diminish what occurred. I think it's best if I just start from the beginning.

It was a beautiful Sunday morning and my self-centered parents decided to ditch me at my grandparents' house; the grandparents on the paternal side.

These grandparents were from the old country, Austria to be exact. They came to the United States penniless to chase the American dream, and by golly, they caught it. For, in the end, they were able to offer their kids a better life than their own. After their retirement they moved into a home on eleven acres of unexplored land with an abundance of squirrels and rabbits and wild turkeys (oh my). It was the only place I was ever let off the leash, on purpose.

They spoke in heavy German accents and served me food in heavy German sauces. I loved going to visit them.

I mention a bit of their background to serve as a stark contrast to the misgivings my parents had about leaving their precious one—me—alone with them. Sure there had already been some "incidents" on previous visits, but nothing serious.

"Are you sure he'll be all right?" my mother asked as my father drove his beloved, rusty Datsun to my grandparents' home.

He adjusted his ridiculous driving gloves, a recent birthday gift, and replied, "I'm pretty sure he'll be okay." It didn't sound convincing.

"Well, have you forgotten the last time we left him there?"

"Listen, if they were able to raise four kids and put them through college, all after coming to this country not speaking a lick of English, I think we can give them one more shot to watch Bo," he said, before adding, "Besides, they're the only ones willing to do it."

I sensed he was trying to convince himself more than my mother.

"Okay. I just want to be sure. By the way, Bo's hair is growing back nicely, isn't it?" It was a quick allusion to my last visit, a few short weeks before.

My father looked back at me, patted my head, and replied, "Yeah, it is. His ears are almost back to normal."

I wish he'd do me a favor and keep his eyes on the road.

During my previous outing, things hadn't gone quite so well. I was chasing vermin in the woods when a ferocious pricker bush attacked me out of nowhere. The bush, with its tentacles full of round, Velcro-like balls, reached out and grabbed me, hanging on for dear life. By the time I escaped its clutches, I was wearing a beautiful burr coat.

I emerged from the wooded area and spotted my grandmother diligently tending to her back garden. She turned to look at me, no doubt expecting to see a beloved companion. What she saw instead was a view of a wild, sixty-three-pound porcupine look-a-like! She jumped to her feet and ran. It wasn't until I whimpered to call her back that she stopped, and from a safe distance realized that the freak of nature sitting there was me.

After failing to get the burrs out of my coat with a brush, she went to the garden shed to get her pruning shears. Snip by snip, she removed the balls of prickery vegetation, right along with copious amounts of my fur. By the time she was done, I was the recipient of the worst haircut ever given to dog, man, or mental patient. Gollum was styling by comparison.

This, at least, explained why her rose bushes never bloomed.

But that was weeks ago and hair grows back. Besides, everytime my parents looked at me with that ridiculous haircut, and I sensed their shame, I successfully hit them up for a treat. Hey, there's a silver lining in every cloud. You just need to know where to look.

When we arrived at their house that fateful day, I jumped out of the car as soon as the door creaked open. I was leashless and free, at least for an afternoon.

Greeting me with his unintentional Arnold Schwarzenegger accent, my grandfather bellowed, "Bo. How ahh yoo?"

That was my cue to say good-bye to my parents and run to the backyard to chase the squirrels that liked to congregate under the picnic table and gossip about the chipmunks that had recently moved into the neighborhood. Once I got bored with chasing the squirrels, I decided to head off into the woods to do some real hunting. Ahh, the great outdoors, this is where animals should be; well, when they're not getting fed leftovers under the dinner table, that is.

Canine Bingo

	B	I	N	G	O
B	Gotta Go Poopie?	Put It Back!	No . . . No!	Stop Barking!	Bad Boy!
I	You're Such A Good Boy	Stop Licking The Cat!	What Would Lassie Do?	Stop Begging!	What Ya Gonna Do Now?
N	Drop It!	Sit . . . I Said Sit!	Free Pass (of Gas)	Want A Treat?	Who Loves Ya?
G	What Ya Got Buddy?	Lay Down!	Leave It!	Stay...hey, I said Stay!	Gotta Go Pee Pee?
O	Go For a Ride?	Stop Licking!	What's That Smell?	What Now?	Go See Mommy!

Number of Players: 2 or more canines

How to Play: Print this sheet out and take it with you wherever you go today. When your owner says one of the comments above, e.g., "Go for a Ride?", find a mud puddle, stick your paw in it, then put your paw print on the square for that comment. The first dog to have mud prints on five across, down, or diagonally is the winner.

Record Holder: Maltball, a diminutive wiener dog, holds the record by completing five across in under three minutes. When let out to go to the bathroom ("Gotta Go Poopie?"), he found a pair of soiled diapers to bring to his father ("Put It Back!") who wanted no part of it (No . . . no!"). After dropping the diaper he told his father how great it smelled and that it was a great gift ("Stop barking!"). All of Maltball's talking got his father in trouble from the neighbors and the canine was swiftly admonished ("Bad boy!").

The daylight was fading faster than I would have liked, but I knew that, this being my Ponderosa, Hop Sing would have some goulash waiting for me back at the ranch. I worked my way home, jumping over old fallen down trees, onto moss-covered rocks, and through dead leaves. Soon the territory became familiar again, my grandparents' house came into view just beyond the trees. The joy of seeing my parents on the back patio enticed me to make my last leap over a dead log a majestic one. I felt like Lassie leaping over a wooden fence in Anytown, USA. Unfortunately, the landing was more Evel Knievel than Baryshnikov. I felt a sharp stabbing sensation in my paw, and although it startled me my focus remained on getting to my parents. That is, until I saw it . . . a lot of it . . . blood! My blood! I came to a screeching halt and examined the source of the throbbing pain. I noticed I had slit open the bottom of my paw, a clean cut straight across my precious paw pad. If one didn't know better, they would have thought I was trying to commit suicide—the slice was that surgical, that precise.

Whoa. I'm getting a little dizzy here just thinking about it. I don't do well with blood, especially if there isn't food involved.

It was clear I needed help, and unfortunately I had to seek it in the form of my parents. I limped across the yard, doing my best not to put undo pressure on my wounded leg. My parents saw me but continued to talk with my grandparents, not taking notice of the hitch in my get-along. I made my limp more pronounced. Helen Keller could have seen it. My parents? Oblivious. They kept gabbing away.

I dragged myself onto the patio and lay down, grateful to have made it that far. My father reached down and patted me on the head, not noticing anything wrong. I wondered whether all humans were this self-involved. Shouldn't someone be giving me a doggy treat?

Before I had a chance to write "Help Me" onto the patio's rough cement with my bloody stump, the cut stopped bleeding. It still throbbed, but as they say in the dog park, "No blood, no fowl." My parents hadn't noticed, so rather than play up the injury here, I vowed to make the most of it when we got home. That's where all the good treats are kept anyway.

I was happy to hear my father say, "We gotta get going." After a quick good-bye, the family packed into the car and headed for the open road home.

"See, I told you he'd be fine. Look, he didn't even get a haircut this time," my father kidded as he merged the car onto the highway.

"I admit that I worry too much. It's just that, I don't know what I'd do if anything ever happened to him," my mother replied.

"I know. I feel the same way."

Then in his dopey, Deputy Dawg voice he turned to me and said, "Hey, buddy, buddy, buddy. We'd never let anything happen to you. Oh . . . no . . . we . . . wouldn't."

If that was the case, why was he going out of his way to hit every pothole on the road? The constant jarring of the car irritated my injury, bump by excruciating bump. I lay down and dangled my paw over the edge of the seat in hopes of minimizing the pain. I closed my eyes, clicked my back two paws together, and repeated to myself, "There's no place like home." Moments later we arrived at our humble abode. Thank you . . . there is a God! behind the curtain after all.

Parked in the garage, the car doors swung open and I was ordered out of the car. A bit dizzy, I was slow to respond. My mother, still unaware anything was amiss, pulled her seat forward to let me out. "C'mon, Bo, let's go."

A second later she shrieked in horror.

I sprang to life as annoying sounds always cause me to do. I jumped out of the car and turned around to see what was wrong this time.

When I saw it I barked in horror, too.

Oh my, what a mess!

There was blood everywhere! In fact, British or not, I'd describe it as a bloody mess. I couldn't help but be reminded of the car scene in *Pulp Fiction*.

My father took a look, and he, too, was shocked, letting out a school girl–type squeal.

My paw must have been bleeding the whole car ride home. No wonder my check engine light was on. They examined me and quickly discovered my wound.

I looked at the two of them and knew my fate rested in their hands. I felt ill.

Since it was a weekend, we'd have to go to the emergency vet rather than my regular doctor. But before we could leave the house my mother insisted that she needed to bandage me up. I'm still not sure if she meant to bandage me up to help stop my blood loss or whether she was afraid of getting more blood on the seats of the car. Yeah, the junky car.

Did I mention I was feeling a little light-headed at this point?

My bloody paw prints had already turned the garage floor into a beautiful shade of crimson by the time my parents ran into the house to frantically search for a bandage.

He searched upstairs and she looked downstairs. Every few seconds they'd yell back and forth to each other on the status of this egg hunt.

"Find anything yet?"

"No"

I waited in the garage, counting down the number of minutes I had left to live. I couldn't believe this was my fate.

"Who doesn't have bandages in their house in case of an emergency?" my father yelled.

"I didn't think we would need them," she yelled back.

"You know, they call them emergencies for a reason."

And the search continued. I lay down, secure in the knowledge that I was going to bleed to death while these two bickered.

I heard them scramble from room to room, rifling through cabinets, drawers, and second aid kits. Then, the old man hit on a brilliant idea. Running into the garage with a roll of paper towels, my father shouted, "I think I got what we need. C'mon, let's go!" My mother came flying through the door moments later, only to shoot him down. "We can't use paper towels. He'll bleed right through them."

Then, as if hit by divine intervention, she exclaimed, "Oh, wait a second . . . I think I know what we can use!"

Seconds later she emerged from the house with the "medical dressing" in her left hand. What she found would have put the average dog in a psychiatric kennel, or at least required some serious counseling. Her brilliant life-saving idea?

A Stayfree maxi pad.

God, please take me now! I thought. Or just cut off my paw and use it as a good luck charm for your key chain. Just don't let her put that thing on me.

My father was as shocked as I was. "We can't put that on him! What will people think?"

"It doesn't matter what people will think. What he needs is help and he needs it now."

"I understand that, but why would you put that on him? Don't we have something . . . smaller?"

"Listen, this is more absorbent than a mini. The wound is pretty big and there is nothing else in the house that will work. Just secure it to his paw with this scotch tape. And be quick about it; we have to get him to the vet!"

I wanted to yell, "Hey, how about using a dish rag or a shirt or even the old man's dirty underwear? I don't know . . . anything but a freakin' maxi pad!" but in my weakened state, all I could do was whimper.

My father shook his head in disbelief and secured the maxi pad on my paw. "If he takes it off, I promise to get his slippers every night," I told myself. But he didn't, and as far as I was concerned he was a lesser man for doing it. Sometimes I wonder which one of us is really neutered.

The old man lifted me into the car and we headed to the emergency room. My mother held my head in her lap, petting it for reassurance even though I continued to get blood all over her "skinny" jeans.

My father turned to me, and in a calm tone said, "Just hold on, little buddy. We're almost there."

I hoped it would be a quiet day at the clinic; then my embarrassment would be minimal. But the number of cars outside suggested otherwise.

My father carried me inside. The main room was full of owners and patients waiting their turn for the vet. As we approached the admissions area, all heads turned simultaneously to watch us.

My father explained what had happened to me, and the nurse behind the desk asked, "What's that on his paw?"

In a whisper, he replied, "That's a maxi pad."

"Why does he have a maxi pad on?" the nurse whispered back.

In a hushed tone, but loud enough for everyone in the waiting area to hear, he responded, "Because they're more absorbent than the mini ones."

My mother flashed him a knowing look of approval.

"Okay then. We're going to take him to the back. While we do please fill this out," the receptionist said, handing him a form.

The vet knocked me unconscious and sewed up my paw. I left with a pink bandage, enough pills to fill a small pharmacy, and a small satellite dish around my head. The only thing they didn't send me home with was my self-respect.

At least I made it out alive.

I will say that my paw feels as good as ever, but a strange thing happens now. Around the same time of every month, my mother gets cranky and my paw starts to throb with pain.

CHAPTER 10

Office Space

One of the downsides of having plenty of food, a warm place to live, and enough money to pay for emergency vet bills is the need for your owners to go to work. Having never been employed, I assumed it was like going to doggy day care where you hang out with a bunch of acquaintances you normally wouldn't have a chance to play with.

Although never officially employed, I'd been tasked with a fair share of work. I was a master gardener, an alarm system, and a bed warmer. I also took out the garbage, helped with the groceries, and acted as a HOV lane dummy on rides with my mother. Come to think of it, I worked more than she did. Maybe she should be the one sitting on the floor instead of me.

Well, as it turned out the old man had the pleasure of working for a Fortune 500 company, making five oats an hour. He toiled away for the man while his life slipped by. He knew it but continued down the well-traveled path anyway in order to support the family.

Prior to finding his way in the world, my father's work history was wide and varied. It included a one-day stint as a dishwasher at a pizzeria, a six-week spell as a telemarketer selling credit card protection, a summer's worth of counting plastic ET heads at the factory where they were produced, and a two-summer stretch as a groundskeeper of an apartment complex. Of course he had been pumping gas for his parents since the age of twelve and the number one gofer of tools for his father in that time frame. But that was all just a warm-up for the big leagues.

His first stint was with a large conglomerate, finishing his assignment in a month's time. Shortly thereafter he was requested to come back and work in their accounting department. A few months went by before he was offered a full-time position to join the firm. So now, several years later, he found himself standing on the second rung of the corporate ladder, looking for a way to get off. But it was already too late.

Long hours at the office during the week were followed by several hours of work on the weekends. It seemed, at times, I hadn't seen my father in weeks.

My mother missed him, too. She'd sit on the couch and tell me that she was feeling a bit lonely. I'd sit there and listen patiently, knowing she would get up shortly and serve herself up some sympathy food.

I was there to help with the crumbs. After a while, my mother's spunk kicked in. I watched her face brighten as she said, "Bo, let's go for a ride!" She loved her rides as much as I did. I never dared bark *ride* for fear of putting her in spastic convulsions. I didn't risk spelling it, either, since she was pretty good at that, too.

While out about town, we'd stop at Burger King or McDonald's to grab a quick burger. If we were near the ice cream stand, we'd hit it up for a baby cone or two.

We were inseparable, until the old man came home.

Then we'd both vie for his attention.

After one notable period of minimal contact, he came home and surprised me; he invited me to join him at the office the following Saturday. Naturally I was surprised, since I didn't know much about general accounting and my business management skills were untested. Salary negotiations would have to wait until I proved my worth. At a minimum I figured I'd be getting a jar of peanut butter a week. That, along with quarterly beef jerky bonuses, would classify me as "rich" by the government.

I woke up that Saturday morning ready to go, but not sure whether the offer was still on the table.

When my father asked, "Hey, buddy, you wanna go to work?" I couldn't believe my ears.

Do I wanna go? Does the cat poop in the house?

Once we arrived at the office complex, my father leashed and escorted me into the building. He signed me in and gave me a badge, and we were off to roam the building.

His office was located on a floor laid out in the typical, bland cube farm that you see in every Dilbert cartoon. My old man was lucky, though; he had an office on the outer wall all to himself. I knew which one it was without ever having been told. It smelled of him, maybe too much so.

I met some of his co-workers who took the opportunity to suck up to me. This told me one of two things: I was to be placed in a position of power or I was damn cute. Who am I kidding? It was probably both.

I put my lunch bag in the refrigerator, a twenty-five-cent piece into the swear jar, and gossiped at the water cooler about Lassie's recent weight gain. Five minutes into the conversation, my father called me to come join him in an area of the office building that was currently being refurnished. I jumped at the opportunity.

The new floor was near completion, with cubicles on the perimeter and conference rooms in the center. The effect of which, intentional or not, created a racetrack setting—perfect for a dog who loves to run. It smelled of new construction, you know, a wood smell coupled with a new carpet smell.

Unexpectedly it also smelled of canine—a Labrador in particular.

I soon learned that the scent belonged to Murphy—a beautiful black Lab, about the same age as me, and he belonged to one of my father's co-workers. We smelled each other's privates; he tried to mount me, I tried to mount him. It was friendship at first smell.

Our owners, seeing that we got along with each other, left us to our own devices and headed back to the main work office. It was just Murph, a few cubicle farmhands, and me on the entire floor.

The racetrack beckoned. When in Rome, or Talladega, do as the Romans do. So Murphy and I ran. A lot.

"Round and round they go, where they'll stop nobody knows," barked the voice in my head. I didn't know why my father hated work so much—this seemed like fun to me! The running continued until it was time to go home.

At the end of that first weekend, I was tired and slept for the next two days. It had felt good supporting the family with my work and I looked forward to getting to the office again. That opportunity came quickly.

Briefcase in one paw, lunch bag in the other, I carpooled with my father to work the following Saturday. As before, I was escorted to the new section of the building and given my instructions.

"Now don't do anything bad while you're here," my father warned. "If you have to go, hold it until I get back."

This place was now mine. I awaited Murphy's arrival so we could "think outside of the box." Maybe this week, we'd chase each other counterclockwise? I had heard that's how the Australian shepherds do it.

Time passed.

Tick. Tock.

Tick . . . tock.

Tick . . . tock.

Hmmm, where was Murph? He hadn't left an out of office message so maybe he had called in sick? I waited some more, but it was clear Murph was a no-show.

This got me to thinking, if Murph wasn't going to be here, then why bring me? What was the old man's motivation? Did he want me to push paper around instead of just running free? Working for a living wasn't so fun, after all.

I was trotting around the racetrack, contemplating the answer when it dawned on me that I hadn't received a message all day. I did another lap to make sure that I hadn't missed any. Sniff. Nada. Sniff. Sniff. Absolutely nothing. No messages at all.

I had read in *Business Week* that companies value employees more if they show leadership skills, so I decided to initiate the exchange of ideas. I raised my leg as high as it could reach and left my first business message, right on the cubicle wall located by the entrance.

If memory serves me correctly, it was a long one.

I continued around the perimeter of the office leaving a note every three or four cubes. It was hard work, especially toward the end; I see why my father was always stressed. I'd be back next week to check for replies.

To help my work stand out, I wanted to create an all employee bulletin with a little more, uhmm, substance. Something that would truly catch their attention.

Then it dawned on me: Why not post the message right in the middle of the racetrack? Why not, indeed!

I finished it off with a Carvel-like swirl. Cookie Puss would have been proud, although no more so than Fudgie the Whale. It was simply a work of art—the finest dump ever taken in an office.

While I admired my handy work, one of the cubicle

dwellers in the area raced to tell my father. Excellent. My memo would not go unnoticed.

He came running into my office with a stern expression on his face. He admonished me and, after finishing his tirade, ended up doing what he had to do.

With his unkempt hair swept across his forehead, he turned to me and said, "You're fired!"

Although some will say I was let go as a result of a poorly communicated memo, I think the decision was based on the fact he did not want me to be in the same pressure-inducing environment he was forced to struggle with on a regular basis.

My father had put an end to my budding career as a business dog, a career that never fully got started, for my own good. I wouldn't have to fire an employee, stress out over big presentations, or worry how fat my ass looked on a photocopy machine. No, I would be able to pursue what I was passionate about: food and sleep.

Man, I loved him for sacrificing his mental well-being for the entire family, and especially for me. In our family, he was the true working-class dog.

Although grateful for being relieved of my duties, I do wonder if anybody ever returned my messages.

CHAPTER 11

Ehh, What's Up, Dog?

My parents don't entertain much. The only people who came to our house were my mother's parents and occasionally Marcy Catcollector with her husband in tow. My father's family rarely visited, and it was almost unheard of for anyone unrelated to stop by, outside of the paper boy looking for payment, that is.

It's not that we're an unsociable family. I suspect the real reason for not inviting people over had more to do with my parents' collective inability to cook a decent meal. In fact, the first meal my mother ever made for my father wasn't made by her at all. No. Her father made it. He prepared the meal beforehand along with printed directions on how to reheat it. One Chicken Cordon Bleu meal later and my old man was hooked on my mother's cooking, all under false pretenses.

There may have been other reasons why my parents didn't invite people often, and I imagine it had to do with the number of pet mishaps that transpired in the presence of guests. Admittedly I had my fair share of incidents, but lest you think I was totally to blame, let me spill the beans on an incident that occurred when my parents invited Marcy Catcollector and her husband over for dinner.

Why they chose to accept the invitation is beyond me.

Maybe they hadn't had their fill of Prince's Macaroni and Cheese lately. Personally, I think powdered cheese gets a bad rap, especially if you've never had the opportunity to lick the bowl afterward. For the uninitiated, it gets all hard and gunky, and doesn't break up easily. It's like a Tootsie Pop for the canine set. How many licks? More than three, that's for sure. Anyway, I love it. Most invited guests don't.

After downing supper, the "dinner party" moved its way into the front living room. This was odd in that this is the room we never hang out in. It has no TV, no rugs, and most importantly, no curtains. I steer clear because I can't bear the thought of licking myself in front of the neighborhood voyeurs. It's not that I'm shy, just that if I'm going to put on a show, I expect a few pepperoni-tasting shekels for it.

As everyone found their spot to sit, including me, it became clear why we were there. My mother went to the armoire and retrieved the photo album she'd recently finished. It held the best collection of pictures ever assembled. Yes, they were snapshots of me in various heroic poses: me peeing on a tree, me peeing on a mailbox, and the iconic, me peeing on a fire hydrant. Brilliant stuff.

Sitting on the love seat next to her husband, Catcollector turned the pages of the album. Every now and again, she'd take an exaggerated sniff of the air until my mother finally asked, "Do you need a tissue?"

"No. Something smells funny in here."

My father took a few sniffs, too. "Yeah, there's something weird about this room. Every once in a while there's a smell. We can't figure out what it is."

They went back to their conversation about how photogenic I was before the subject of the smell arose again.

"There's that smell. Where's it coming from?" Catcollector asked.

By this time she was on the floor looking under the couch.

Favorite Non-Food Smells

 Dog butt

 Cat butt

 My own butt

 Dead chipmunks in the yard

 My mother's perfumed body

 My father's B.O.

 Napalm in the morning

 Broccoli farts (hmmm . . . isn't that a food smell?)

 Teen spirit

 My pee on anything

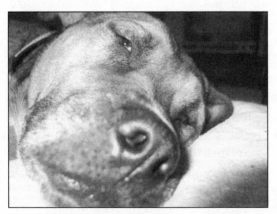

I don't smell a darn thing right now.

My mother and father played along, getting on the floor, too. Mr. Catcollector followed suit.

All four were now at eye level, something I was used to with other dogs in my life. The strange thing about this situation wasn't that humans were on all fours, but that nobody tried to sniff my privates. This was a dinner party, after all. How rude.

They continued to scour the area and found nothing.

"I don't smell it anymore," Catcollector said as she got up off her knees.

I knew the source of the smell, in fact I had known for a long time, but figured I'd let them figure it out on their own. I've noticed humans' self-esteem rises when they discover things by themselves. Who am I to tear them down?

When Catcollector and her husband plopped themselves back down on the loveseat, the smell wafted through the room.

"I think it's the couch!" Marcy yelled.

"Uhmm, you've been sitting in cat piss. Of course it smells," I barked.

She ignored me as she stuck her nose into the couch cushions.

"It's cat pee!"

The other three heads, in unison, bowed toward the couch to confirm that yes; it was unsweetened Moose lemonade.

Unbeknownst to anyone, weeks earlier Moose had taken a liking to that one piece of furniture. It was a love seat, and she loved to pee on it, making it the best-smelling piece of Sears furniture we had. There were many reasons why Moose and I got along so well. Uninhibited peeing was just one of them.

The next day, the vet concluded she may have had a bladder infection but that it had resolved quite a while ago, so it wasn't the cause of her peeing anymore. It was now just a habit, something that my parents would try to break for the next several years.

I watched as they bought rolls of aluminum foil to put over the couch. And I watched Moose swat away the sheets just before lowering her tush and piddling on the cushions.

I watched as my parents put the kitty litter box on the love seat, in hopes that Moose would pee in it. And I watched as Moose conveniently lowered her tush to wee just outside of it.

I watched as strangers came with their cleaning machines in an attempt to remove the smell. And I watched as Moose lowered her tush and sprayed her perfume on it after they left. That had me in stitches every time.

Over the years, some of my father's friends slept on the couch after a night out on the town. They'd wake up smelling like urine, with cat hair on their clothes and kitty litter indentations on their face. When the family finally said goodbye to the love seat, it was like an old friend leaving town. I was sad to see it go.

I always go back to that night and think, What if the guests had been my father's boss or worse, the owners of the cute Lab from down the road? We could have ended up penniless or worse, me without a prom date.

I, too, had shown a propensity for inappropriate behavior. On different occasions I had mounted a guest's leg, thrown up on a visitor's shoe, and pulled a tasty snot rag out of a pocketbook. Anything was possible and I imagine that if my parents had adopted a dingo instead of me, it would probably have eaten one of their guest's babies. That was just their luck.

So my parents were a bit gun-shy in having people over and rightfully so. That's why it was a surprise when they decided to invite both sides of the family over for a Fourth of July cookout.

I knew a cookout meant not only ample begging opportunities on behalf of clueless relatives, but also plentiful chances to escape. I counted down the days until the festive occasion.

The doorbell rang. The first to arrive were the Cat-collectors. They steered clear of the living room and quickly made their way to the back deck. A constant stream of family members made their way into the house, each with their own unique smell. I evaluated each one, trying to determine who had the most prolific treat-giving potential.

I landed on a sure thing when my grandmother on my mother's side walked through the door. This was a woman who'd devour a brick of old, moldy cheese in the middle of the night, and when confronted the next morning say, "Yeah I ate it, but it wasn't very good." She was a food-finding machine and liberal in dispensing it to me. In my book, that's a keeper. I stayed close to her all day.

The cookout was in full swing and I was in full begging mode when I spotted Bugs off in the distance. He knew I saw him and I knew he knew. It was a game we had been playing for a while. He taunted me, flicking his little bunny tail, knowing full well I was confined to the back deck by a baby gate. I smelled him, I saw him, and I wanted him. Bad, real bad.

I had to keep my cool; I was in the middle of a social gathering, after all. So on the outside, I was wagging my tail and smiling, but on the inside, I was all tied up in knots. You'd think that with all the grandparents and siblings on hand, the constant flow of traffic in and out of the patio door would present a grand escape opportunity, but no luck. I hung around the door, thinking, If only one of these dopes would make the mistake of opening that gate, the rabbit will be mine.

Regrettably, my mother had issued persistent warnings to all guests not to open the baby gate for any reason, thus blocking my way to that smart-ass bunny. Not deterred, I looked for alternatives.

First I scoped out the deck railing. It looked like I couldn't even get my big head through the slats, and even if I could, there was a ten-foot drop to deal with. I like pain about as much as I do onions, so that choice was out.

I scoured the options inside the house. Front door: closed. Back door to the garage: closed. First floor windows: closed.

Resigned to defeat, I focused on other things, namely begging for food. This always calms my nerves. After scoring some cheese and crackers, I headed back outside to check if my nemesis was still around. Sure enough, Bugs was sitting there, laughing at me again, just laughing. Didn't he realize he was pulling on Underdog's cape?

This got my juices flowing. I squirmed and whined like a puppy that just had its first shoe taken away, letting Bugs know that I was onto him. But the whinier I got, the more he heckled me.

Then he upped the ante and hopped within ten feet of me. Ten feet! Well, in reality it was really 14.14 feet using the Pythagorean theorem (10 feet up, 10 feet across = 14.14 feet to rabbit stew), but you get the picture.

I couldn't take it anymore! I lost my mind. I forgot about the guests, and the party, and my parents. I took a few steps back, turned, and sprinted toward the rabbit, oblivious to anything in my way. I think I may have hit some elderly legs and a chair or two before I crashed into the deck railing. To my amazement, it did nothing to hinder my momentum, and before I knew it, I was airborne.

Shrieks of terror came from the partygoers as I sailed out over the backyard. I felt just like Underdog, and much like him, I was on a mission to stop evil. It wasn't to save Sweet Polly Purebred from that vile Simon Barsinister, but rather to sink my teeth into one Bugs Bunny, certified wiseass.

I hit the ground hard and rolled to a stop. I pawed the major parts of my body to make sure nothing was broken. Astonishingly, I had made it through unharmed and gave chase.

Bugs took off like a shot. He wasn't laughing anymore. I heard my parents calling me from the deck, but I couldn't turn back until I accomplished my mission.

The pursuit lasted the remainder of the day. I barked relentlessly to alert my parents that I was okay but still on the hunt. Into the woods, through the creek, and out the drainage pipes I went, following wherever his smell would take me. It was nice to be on a hunt and to be free again. I recall thinking, This is what free range chickens must feel like.

I returned home later that evening without Bugs, covered in burrs, sticks, and sewage goo. I knew I was in for a "torture bath" from my father, but it was worth it, like they always are.

Bugs never did come back to taunt me. One encounter with a flying dog must have been enough to keep him away for life.

You know who else never came back? Most of our guests.

But as I went to sleep that night I pondered about my few hours of freedom and realized, that on this day, July 4, everyone should remember what a great privilege it is to be in this country and free.

A great privilege, that is, if you aren't a dog confined by a baby gate.

CHAPTER 12

Vacation House

We all need a break, whether it's a break from the mundane, the necessary, or each other. Time away gives us perspective, improves our mental well-being, and keeps our tails wagging.

When my parents hear the word *vacation* they think about seaside cottages, lazy afternoons spent reading, and penny candy. But before they make their great escape, they must ask themselves a very important question: "What are we going to do with Bo?"

When I think of a vacation, I think of long walks in the woods, eyeballing Chihuahuas on the beach, and chowing down at all you can eat turkey jerky buffets. But my parents never think of sending *me* on vacation. Instead, they send me to the home of an unsuspecting do-gooder who has volunteered to dog-sit while they live it up.

But it's not all bad. Do-gooders are suckers, and that allows me to showcase my well-honed tricks of the doggie trade to the rest of the world. And beg for table scraps. Once the word *vacation* is uttered, a canine's well-being becomes secondary to trip planning and packing. As much as my parents love me, my house is no different. The night before the trip is a flurry of activity. The old man fills his suitcase with ten-year-old T-shirts while my mother fills hers with recently purchased vacation outfits. My bag is filled with a leash, a container of food, and a ratty old blanket.

Heaven forbid I want to go for a walk or get some extra snuggle time. It's not in the cards the night before an official outing.

I remember the first time I heard the word vacation. I'd been with my family for several months and during that time never spent more than a few hours outside of their company. We were a pack that did everything together; I assumed this was the way it would always be. I soon found out otherwise.

They were headed to the coast of Maine, where the cool water and warm summer breeze beckoned visitors from hundreds of miles around.

However, they needed to find a place for me to "chill" for a few days, in addition to securing reliable transportation to their destination. Even though they were both responsible adults in their late twenties, they still owned vehicles that were unreliable for trips over fifty miles.

They soon came up with the perfect plan. They would drop me off at my aunt Heidi and uncle Bob's house, and in the process borrow one of their cars, preferably the fast sporty one. After a quick phone call, the deal was done.

The way I saw it, I was the down payment to ensure the car was coming back.

To the untrained eye, this didn't look like a bad plan. But it was. You see, my to-be dog-sitters were the owners of the infamous Mickey, known on the streets as McDuff. He was their beloved, yet demented, black Scottish terrier that was afflicted with wild mood swings. He was bipolar, spending the preponderance of time south of the border.

I was furious. My parents had sold me out for a sports car, knowing full well they were leaving me with a psychopathic ball of wiry fur.

Lest you think I'm overreacting, let me tell you a little bit about McDuff.

McDuff's legacy was cemented in family folklore exactly one Christmas Eve prior to my arrival in the pack. His mental disorder was well known within the family circle, and the advice given to everyone who encountered him was to treat him just like you treat people in NYC. Don't make direct eye contact unless you want trouble.

My father didn't heed the warning, mostly because it came from my mother.

He approached McDuff with treat in hand.

As he bent over to give it to him, McDuff saw his opportunity. The terrier jumped chest high and snagged his eyetooth on the wooly yarn of my father's brand-new Christmas sweater. As my father straightened up, McDuff dangled from his sweater, just like a newly hung doggie Christmas ornament.

McDuff swung there for a solid minute, growling all the while, before anyone was able to release him from the old man's holiday top. To this day my aunt apologizes for her dog's actions.

Scottish terrier: $500, box of biscuits: $4, the look on your father's face with a growling dog hanging from his sweater: priceless. I wish I could have been there.

So my mother was terrified of this dog, and he had attacked my father, but they had no problem leaving me alone with him just so they could go on their precious vacation.

Why couldn't they just have sent me to the Poop 'n' Play doggie camp instead?

On the day of their departure it was as if my parents had forgotten they were even pet owners. They dropped me off and were gone in a flash, driving a sporty two-seat dream machine to paradise. The only evidence they had been there was the late '70s rice burner we had arrived in. It was sitting in the driveway, right next to the house that would be my home for the next few days.

I followed my aunt and uncle into their home. As we got closer to the door, I could smell the warning signs.

On the tree was "McDuff Lives Here," by the rose bush was "Pee Here and Die," and on the fence post was the ominous, "Want to Save a Lot on Your Canine Insurance? Dial 1-800-Run-Now!"I had a bad feeling, but it was too late to turn around. Besides, where would I go?

I was standing inside the entrance of the enclosed back porch when I noticed the unmistakable outline of a Scottish terrier in the kitchen doorway. His black face melded into the blackness of his body. His two marble eyes followed my every move, while the whiteness of his teeth became more evident with every step I took. True to the advice given me, I didn't make direct eye contact. I just kept walking, keeping close to my aunt's legs, through the kitchen and into the living room.

I smelled his odor everywhere; this was clearly McDuff's turf.

I admit, I was intimidated, and from the deep recesses of my mind I kept hearing a message my father had given me: "If you don't punch the bully in the nose first, he's going to do it to you." He was referring to the "dachshund incident," during which a hot dog–shaped canine stole my plush doggie bone from under my nose, but the advice seemed appropriate here, too. I needed to hit McDuff in the snout with the best weapon I had.

As many know, the first thing learned in male puppy school is to leave your mark (it's also the last thing you learn). Before you know it, it's second nature. I liken it to human kids texting on their phones. At first it's unnatural, but pretty soon it's all they know how to do.

So I staked my own territory; an island nation in the Land

of McDuff. Raising my leg high up on the couch, I peed my name on it. The couch with the big B and O on it was now mine. I finished before my aunt could stop me. I was fortunate to have such a short name.

Even though I was a guest, they frowned upon my actions, admonished me, and led me out the front door to finish my pee.

Upon my return McDuff showed me he was a worthy adversary. Although fully housebroken, he reclaimed his territory by peeing on the couch in the exact spot where I had soiled it. He only managed to get out an M, shaped like the Golden Arches, before being scolded by his father. Evading capture, he darted to the middle of the living room and squeezed out a dump right in front of his parents. It was quick; he didn't even bother to bring reading material.

Clearly he wasn't amused by my presence.

Having lived with McDuff for years, his owners knew enough to keep us apart. He was gated in the kitchen while I was allowed to roam in the living room. I investigated the surroundings by taking in the aroma of the carpet (they had a cat), smelling the couch cushions (somebody liked cabbage), and looking out the window (somebody could use an edger).

After I finished exploring, I stared at my captors waiting for the fun to begin.

I conveyed to them, "C'mon, this is your chance to hang with the Bo Monster. What are we gonna do?"

They just sat there, looking at the TV.

It was like giving someone the chance to hang with Wonder Dog only to have them say, "No thanks, I'm going to take a nap."

I whined with displeasure for the remainder of the day.

As the day came to a close, it was time to be let out to

do our business. McDuff was first; he was the incumbent dog after all. As my aunt and uncle opened the door to let him out, I noticed they weren't paying attention to me at all, presenting me with the perfect opportunity to make a break for it. What a bunch of amateurs! These people call themselves dog owners?

I bolted through their legs, past the open door, and out into the open neighborhood. I was free!

I sprinted around to the front of the house and down the dark suburban street. They yelled frantically for me to come back, but I only ran faster and faster, thinking, Run, Forrest, run!

When I was comfortably distant from the cries of anguish, I eased into a slow trot and then a meandering walk.

Going from yard to yard, I smelled the remnants of Purina One—natural blend, Eukanuba-premium performance formula, and a variety of Bil-Jac treats. It was clear I was in a nicer part of town than I was used to. As the voices continued calling my name in the distance, I focused on the task at hand: finding out how the other half lived. Did you know that some dogs don't even eat commercial dog food, others drink only bottled water, while still others take antidepressant medication to get them through the day? I know, it's sad.

I was having so much fun with my detective work I didn't want to be caught. When the voices got near, giving my keepers a glimmer of hope of corralling me, I'd take off and vanish into the darkness. Wash, rinse, and repeat until their spirit was crushed.

It took a while, but once their will was broken, my aunt and uncle gave up the pursuit. By this time I, too, was finished with my pursuit for information, and shadowed their retreat back to the "vacation" home. I could only hope the turn-down service had put chocolates on my pillow.

I stood outside the front door ready to bark my arrival back home when I heard my aunt repeating, "Oh, my God, we lost their dog! Oh . . . my . . . God . . . we *lost* their dog!"

I could see her pacing through the sidelights of the doorway. My uncle sat on the couch with his head in his hands. He spoke in a distant voice as if he were recounting a painful memory. "I tried to get him. I really did but everytime I got close he just took off. I almost had him two or three times. He'd lure me in and then, just when I thought I had him, he'd take off. I think I heard him laughing at me."

"Do you have any idea where he is now? Please tell me you do!" my aunt pleaded.

"I have no idea. The last I saw of him, he was a few blocks away, running behind everybody's house."

"Oh, my God, what am I going to tell my brother when he calls us? We *lost* his dog!"

I sat there giggling with delight. I love to see humans sweat; it makes them easier to track. Maybe this would teach these two to be more outgoing when they have four-legged guests to entertain.

This conversation was so delicious my nose was pressed against the sidelight. I didn't even notice McDuff on the other side, staring back at me. The jig was up, or so I thought, but McDuff didn't bark a peep.

He turned around, sat, and watched the show. Apparently he was enjoying it just as much as me.

It wasn't long before I'd had enough. It was a long day and it was best to get a good night's rest. I announced my return with, "Woof! Woof!"

"What was that?"

"I think it's him! He's back!" They ran to the front door and opened it. There I stood with my black tongue hanging out, between two lips in the shape of a grin.

"Bo, come here! You scared us to death. Oh, Bo, you're

back! He's back!!" My aunt fussed as she hugged me and pulled me into the house. I like a good family reunion.

McDuff gave me a wink to show me he appreciated a good escape, and certainly one that put his owners in such a tizzy.

It was near midnight now, so we were all ushered upstairs to the main bedroom. My aunt, uncle, and McDuff shared the bed while the ancient cat and I slept on the floor. We all dreamed pleasant dreams.

All of us, that is, except the evil one among us.

In the middle of the night I was awakened by a loud scream. "Oww, my toe. Oh, my toe!" yelled my uncle.

The scream woke my aunt. "What is it? What's wrong?"

"McDuff. He bit my toe! That son of a bitch bit my toe!"

Showing the same amount of concern as my mother would, my aunt said, "Well you were probably moving your feet too much. You must have been bothering him."

I looked up at the bed, and there McDuff lay looking directly back at me. In the dim light of the alarm clock, I swear I saw him smile.

I gave him a wink for a job well done and went back to bed.

The next day, my aunt removed the gate that separated me from McDuff. We were members of a common cause, that of the "resistance." He had my back and I had his.

Later, my mother called from Maine to check on me. Apparently my parents had a little bit of Bo separation anxiety. My aunt answered the phone in the kitchen and said, "Bo is doing great. He's such a good dog. Why no, he hasn't been any trouble at all. Mickey and him are getting along really well." Then, a few moments later I heard her say, "So we should be careful when we open the door? He'll run out? He hasn't tried to yet but we'll make sure to be careful. Don't worry, we're dog parents. We know how to handle him."

I lay on the floor, just outside the kitchen, nibbling on one of my uncle's fine leather loafers. Oh these people were dog parents all right, just not very good ones.

My newfound respect for McDuff coupled with my aunt and uncle watching me like a hawk resulted in an uneventful couple of days. When not on a walk or car ride, I got bored and whined my displeasure as often as I could.

My bond with McDuff strengthened over the next few days. I let him take the lead around the food bowl, he let me take the lead on our walks, and we alternated dibs on the fire hydrants we passed. I realized he wasn't such a bad guy, just misunderstood.

The purring of a finely tuned sports car announced my parents' return from Maine. I jumped up and down in front of the living room window, barking like a high maintenance poodle on speed and caught a glimpse of my father proudly parking the car. I ran to the back windows and stood on my hind legs to watch my parents exit the car.

They looked happy, but not as happy as my aunt and uncle seemed at my imminent departure. I could hear my smiling mother ask, "How was he?"

"He was no trouble at all. Come in for a few minutes," my aunt replied.

"McDuff didn't bite him, did he?"

"No. They were both really good. Bo was so much fun to be around. I think they're good buddies now."

"We're so glad. We were so worried about him."

"Oh, anytime you guys want to leave him here, we'll be more than happy to take him." It was a good thing my aunt wasn't hooked up to a lie detector.

After my parents presented gifts as a gesture of thanks, we made our way to my parents' car. I jumped into the backseat, ready to head home.

My Ten Favorite Foods

1. *Drive-Thru Burger King*   The #1, no pickles, extra cheese, super-sized.

2. *Garbage Pail Surprise*   You know not what you get when you flip the lid.

3. *Anything concocted in Moose's oven*   Baked with love.

4. *Iams cat food*   Made with that special ingredient that always makes things taste better . . . it's called NotForMe Spice.

5. *Duck à l'orange*   Preferably Daffy.

6. *Caramel macchiato*   Venti—with an almond croissant

7. *Kreature Komfort baked goods*   Mailmen on a stick rule.

8. *Frozen Paws ice cream*   Be careful of the brain freeze.

9. *Peanut butter*   In a jar, on a spoon, or in a Kong.

10. *Pizza crust*   Cold, hold the anchovies.

The aftermath of a serving of Garbage Pail Surprise

As we backed out of the driveway, my relieved aunt and uncle stood in front of my vacation home waving good-bye.

I barked, "Don't worry. I'll make sure to be back next year."

CHAPTER 13

Walk Hard

My mother always says, "Walks with Bo are like a box of chocolates. You never know what you're gonna get."

To which my father always replies, "You just need to hold on to his leash tighter."

He has a point. My mother lacks the leash control my father possesses. When I walk with him I always know he is in charge. If I take off to chase something, he yanks the leash back, pretty near decapitating me.

They each have their own styles, with one lending itself to mayhem while the other lends itself to control. You can guess which I prefer. Yep, mayhem. Every time.

Early one Saturday, I awoke and detected a strange aroma wafting through the single pane windows. Snow? Could it be? I jumped off the bed onto the floor and stuck my head between the curtains to look outside. Sure enough it had snowed the previous night. Snow!

There wasn't a single thing in the world I loved more than snow. Not Moose, not my parents, not even farting in bed. No, snow was the end all and be all for me.

This particular snowfall had blanketed the roads and trees with a thick coat of marshmallow fluff, the type chiropractors love: wet and heavy. It was also USDA grade A quality for those who like writing their name in Mother

Nature's dandruff, which of course I did. I especially liked decorating the O in my name with a smiley face. The locals loved that, too.

Oh, boy! A fun day lay before me; it was time to motivate the family into action.

Target number one: the old man. He's the fun one who chases me, roughhouses with me, and generally treats me like the manly dog I am. Unfortunately, trying to wake him is like trying to wake a bear in the winter. Don't do it unless you're prepared to have your snout ripped off.

My mother on the other hand is a light sleeper, but regrettably, light on the touch, too.

I'd take my chances with him.

I jumped on the bed and licked my father's face. He just rolled over. Not deterred I stuck my nose under his body, nudging him the best I could. My mother took notice of my excitement and tried to help my cause. "Honey, he's trying to tell you something."

Faking sleep, my father just lay there.

"I know you can hear me, Bo wants to go out and play. Get up." He didn't move. Maybe he was hibernating or died in his sleep. I ran to get a mirror to put under his nose, but before I could, my mother acquiesced, "Okay, I'll do it this morning. But it's your job tomorrow."

My father rolled over, indicating his life force, as weak as it may have been, was still within him. He manipulated my mother almost as well as I did.

Reluctantly my mother got up and put on her winter garb. At the sight of the layers of snow on the ground, she groaned. I, on the other hand, howled with youthful glee at the quantity covering our front stoop.

When she opened the door I sprinted outside. A few seconds later my paws felt the cold, white crystals between my furry toes, but that didn't deter me from circling my mother, barking the whole time. "Come on, chase me. You know you want to. Chase me!"

No matter how much I tried to encourage her, she just wasn't in the mood. Granted she hadn't had her coffee yet, but this was snow we were talking about. I could tell by her body language she was intent on making this one of those short treks down the street and back.

I looked for an opportunity to change that.

Just around the corner, she started pressuring me to do my business. I was about to bark, "Hey, we're not even at the end of the road!" when fate intervened. It was in the form of a pack of kids off in the distance, sledding.

I jumped into action by initiating the game of Slip the Leash. You may have seen the board version at the local PetSmart, but for those not well versed in canine subculture it's an easy game to play. Pull forward on the leash and then pull your head back on the dog collar. Pull forward, pull back. Do it again, and again. Before you know it, your head will pop out of your collar and you're free. It's a great game. Highly recommended. I give it five milk-bones out of five.

My mother fell for this trick every time, leaving her holding a leash with a collar but no dog, and this time was no different.

Once free, I ran toward the kids with my screaming mother trailing behind. She didn't have a chance of catching me; she ran as if her boots were tied together. The closer I got the clearer I could make out my new play buddies. They looked a rowdy bunch with fun on their minds, and best of all they were only slightly larger in stature than me.

I spotted a little tubby boy in a deep red snowmobile suit sledding down the hill. I don't think they make those anymore; the snowmobile suit, that is. They still make tubby little boys. I ran to meet Tubby. I wanted in on his Arctic Express.

I jumped toward him and, as Emeril would say, *"Bam!"* a massive collision.

Tubby went flying off his sled while I flew in the other direction. What a hit! I got up and thanked him for playing with plentiful licks to his face. Unfortunately, Tubby's pain threshold was that of a two-year-old, although he was four times that age. He whimpered like a three-month-old puppy that just had his flossy taken away.

My mother caught up to the action. Not happy, she grabbed the scruff of my neck, secured the collar, and pulled me home.

A woman emerged from the home closest to the action. She yelled to my mother, "Hey. Is that your dog that just attacked my son?!"

My mother responded, "Of course it's my dog. Why do you think I have him on a leash?"

Then she took a less confrontational tone. "He was just playing. He doesn't have a mean bone in his body. He broke free when he saw your son going down the hill. He just wanted to play."

"Well, you need to hold on to his leash tighter," came the terse reply.

My mother slinked away, with me in tow. Man, I loved walking with her!

Lest you think it was just the winter walks that were trouble, summer had its share of issues, too, especially if a certain neighbor was in the area.

So it was on a warm summer evening. The sun set in the distance, closing the curtains on a gorgeous day. The disappearing light signaled my evening walk was about to commence. I grew anxious with anticipation, eager to find out what had changed in the neighborhood since the morning. My mother donned her ten-dollar Keds (for this was a moment she felt like a pro), secured my leash, and headed out the door.

Down the stoop I ran, straining at my lead, when out of the corner of my eye, I saw our neighbor Monty walking down the street.

He didn't own a dog; he just liked walking himself instead. I knew if we didn't get out front quickly this chance encounter would turn my long walk into a short one. He was the neighborhood windbag, and once involved in a conversation with him, escape was near impossible. You might as well be a white mouse trying to unravel yourself from a python.

When my mother spotted him, she picked up the pace, making sure to only look at the pavement directly in front of her.

Then, from a distance I heard, "Bobo! Is Mommy giving you a walk tonight?"

The python had spotted us.

Social mores forced my mother to stop and wait for him to catch up.

"Nice night for a walk, isn't it?" Monty asked as he came upon us.

Was a night for a nice walk would have been more appropriate, but I kept my mouth shut.

"Yes it is," my mother replied.

The python had her in his grasp. He slinked his body around her.

He asked, "Did you hear about Julie and Ken down the road?"

Submitting to his will, my mother played along. "No, what?"

"Apparently they're having problems with their son.

From what I've heard he was arrested last night for . . ."
Yada, yada, yada.

The python had started his squeeze.

Every once in a while my mother—the mouse—would squeak, "I really should get going. Bo really needs his walk."

To which the python would reply, "Yeah, he could use some exercise. You know who else could use some exercise? Helen from down the street. I don't know if you noticed but she's getting pretty heavy." And on he would go.

The mouse could barely breathe.

While listening to this, I impatiently circled the two while my mother stepped over the lead, moved the leash from one hand to the other, passed it around her back; all in sync with my activity. It was like a mating dance performed by some little known species in Africa that tasted like something yummy. Something like mailman shaped gingerbread cookies from a warm oven.

But fate was about to intervene, whether it was fortunate or not is up for debate.

It all started with the unique tingling sensation that signaled my superpowers activating; some call this a sixth sense, I call it Miss Cleo Vision. It warned of an intruder in the area.

I lifted my nose and sniffed the air, and it wasn't long before I spotted him, sitting in the distance. It was a squirrel, most likely on a fifteen-minute break from the nut factory and completely oblivious to me. This was my chance to kill two birds with one bark. I'd save my mother from the python and get me some exercise time in the process.

I ended the dance with my mother and took off on a full sprint toward the squirrel.

"I think he sees something," Monty observed as I dashed away.

The movement caught my mother off guard; the leash

wrapped around her legs. The friction of the leash inten-
sified, causing me to turn around just in time to see the nylon
rope, tightened into a trip wire, take the legs out from underneath my mother. I didn't wait to see her fall, but I did
hear the sound of plastic hitting her head. It's like the
sound of a Tonka truck after it's dropped from ten feet.

As I got closer to my prize, the squirrel caught a glimpse
of me and quickly ran up the factory steps and into the
tree. I barked and barked but even the supervisor refused
to open the tree house door.

When I looked back, I saw my mother in the road, lying
on her back. She was holding her face with one hand and
the back of her legs with the other.

Monty? He was speechless.

The following night I was let out to do my business. I
heard a familiar voice in the distance say, "Did you hear
what happened to Bo's mother the other night? No? Well
let me tell you she needs to hold on to that leash a little
tighter because . . ." Yada, yada, yada.

The python had his next meal.

CHAPTER 14

Air Supply

"That is disgusting!" my mother cried.

It was an accusatory statement aimed right at the old man as we all lay in bed one night.

"It wasn't me. It really wasn't!" my offended father said. "Nobody pulled my finger, and besides, I didn't try to pull the covers over your head."

"Well, there's only two of us and I know it wasn't me," my mother retorted.

My father sat up, looked my mother in the eyes, and said, "Need I remind you of an era long gone by, where one fine young lady, lying in front of a fan, did unspeakable things?"

My mother couldn't help but giggle.

It was a story my father loved to tell, if only because it was the antithesis of my mother's beliefs on proper social behavior. It goes something akin to the following.

One hot, summer evening my parents had downed a heaping pile of greasy Chinese food. After dinner, they went back to my father's non–air conditioned apartment. It wasn't long before my mother started feeling ill. She lay down on his bed, turning on the fan behind her to try to cool off. It was at this point she let loose with a barrage of SBDs (silent but deadly farts) aimed directly at my father, who sat innocently at his desk doing work.

He smelled it but wasn't sure where it came from. Surely his wife-to-be wouldn't be one to fart in front of him. Besides, she was already asleep. Maybe it was just a figment of his imagination, he thought.

Then the aroma got stronger and stronger.

Maybe he had stepped in some dog poo? He checked his sneakers. Nope. Then he checked his fiancée's shoes. Nothing there, either.

It wasn't until the next day he figured out what happened. When he brought up the unusual smell from the previous night, my mother started laughing uncontrollably. He pressed her on this; she finally fessed up that she was faking sleep and couldn't stop farting. It was the Chinese food, she assured him, and it wouldn't happen again.

It was an ace in the old man's deck of life cards that he pulled out often, especially on occasions during which the air quality in the house was less than perfect.

"Well, do I need to remind you of that time, honey?" he asked again.

"Well if it's not you, and it isn't me, then who is it?" questioned my mother.

Their eyes met for a moment before simultaneously moving on to me.

"Ewe! Bo!" they blurted out while covering their noses.

Guilty, as charged. And to prove it, I let another one squeak by the goalie.

"You reek!" my mother exclaimed.

"Reek" was a little harsh, for this specific fart vintage had a nice bouquet. It was like a fine wine, specially aged for them to enjoy. Could she not smell the love?

No she couldn't. "Bo, you don't live in a barn. Get down. Get down right now!"

I jumped down to sleep the night away on the floor knowing I should have held off on that extra helping of sauerkraut. Even so, I thought the offense should have been treated as a misdemeanor rather than the felony conviction handed down.

But I vowed not to let it bother me. Not on this special night. Not on the night before the annual get-together at Thatcher Park with friends and humans. You see, the following day was my Christmas, my Kwanzaa, my Festivus all wrapped up in a hot dog casing. It was something I looked forward to all year long. It held the promise of food, companionship, and more food.

This wasn't the standard mother, father, me get-together. No, this was an all-day butt-smelling event with a slew of my friends and their owners. These were the type of friends where you can let your hackles down and be yourself.

I couldn't wait for morning to come and the day to begin.

We got up early, packed our supplies, and headed to the park.

Thatcher Park sits high on a heavily treed, mountainous ridge overlooking our small city. The abundance of trails and fresh air leads many a tourist to wander these hills. The smart ones bring their dogs. Even though beautiful, the park's terrain is dangerous. A friend of the family actually fell off the side of the cliff. It was a dog's barking that alerted folks to his misfortune. He was lucky that the limbs of several trees broke his fall, like Rambo. While rehabbing after the accident, he adopted a cat. Clearly the accident had taken a devastating toll on his mental abilities.

I only hoped my parents were careful while there.

I stuck my head out the open window and sucked in the fresh mountain air as we neared our destination. Soon we found our spot and parked in a gravelly parking lot next to an open field. My buddies had already arrived.

BAD TO THE BONE

There was Zack, a black Lab; Betsy, a beagle, and old man Lou. I don't know what breed he was; pups today would call him a hybrid.

I sprang from the car to greet them. My joyful welcome was somewhat subdued by the leash holding me back.

We'd been doing this for a few years now, and it wasn't long before the four-legged of us discussed the begging strategy for the day.

I'd be the loud one, diverting attention, while Zack and Betsy would steal food from the table. Lou would rest under the table and wait for us to bring him his well-deserved due. (Canines respect their elders; of course that's after we beat them up to move them down the pecking order. But hey, once there, we give them their due.)

The good news was that when not being walked, we were tied to the picnic table. That's the thing that holds the food. Damn, I loved this day!

The ten or so humans in attendance did their thing. The men drank and played home run derby in the open field while the women drank and made fun of them.

We lay in the shade of the table, waiting for chips and potato salad to come our way. I took a pass on the sauerkraut. Soon, the first batch of hot dogs and hamburgers were ready, but quickly scarfed down by the humans. A second batch was cooked up. Predictably it was mostly for us, because the area of the human brain responsible for portion control doesn't work when they're in large groups. It's a natural law and every dog knows it.

Laws have consequences, and this time was no different. I was full, very full. I lay on my back staring down at my belly and couldn't help but think it looked like Cool Hand Luke's after fifty eggs. I relaxed by the picnic table digesting my meal while watching the men entertain themselves.

They had gotten tired of softball and were now devising a new game centered around golf. The men took a garbage barrel and moved it to the middle of the open field, about thirty yards away from where I was tied up. From their cars they produced an iron golf club and some golf balls. They created a game with a simple objective; just hit a golf ball into the barrel. If someone managed to do it, all the other players had to chug their beers. I know, very mature, especially for thirty-somethings.

While the game was being set up, my father came over to pet me. He rubbed my belly and was shocked at its size. "Bobo we need to put you on a diet." I looked at his stomach and barked, "After we put you on one."

As quickly as he had come, he left to join the group of men in their reindeer games.

Although they thought they were athletically gifted, their quest to get a golf ball into the barrel proved otherwise. In fact, they never came close.

I heard my mother chiding the guys. "I could do better than that!"

Heck, she couldn't do worse. She kept pressing her point until she was "invited" to give it a try.

My father was obliged to show her how to swing the golf club. After some quick instruction, complicated by the fact my mother was a lefty, he stepped away. Everyone watched to see if she could hit the ball and get it close to the barrel. Even I took my eyes off the field mouse that was now taunting me about my fat belly to see what would happen.

My mother was focused, concentrating hard on the white dimpled ball. As she took the club back into her backswing she looked like an LPGA pro. At the top of the swing she kept her left arm perpendicular to the ground and her right arm cocked at a right angle . . . just like she had been shown. As she started the downward acceleration of her

Ask the Magic Bo Ball*

(Sample Questions and Answers Below)

Question	*Answer*
Am I adorable?	Signs point to yes.
Am I stubborn?	Yes—definitely.
Am I going to heaven?	Reply hazy, try again.
Am I smarter than my parents?	Without a doubt.
Can the fence in the backyard keep me inside?	My sources say no.
Is it true that cats are not as bright as dogs?	As I see it, yes.
Am I the alpha dog in my family?	You may rely on it.
Will I get some of my mother's dinner?	Concentrate and ask again.
What are my chances for a walk today?	Outlook not so good.
Am I in charge?	It is decidedly so.
What is my dog food made of?	Better not tell you now.
Is my e-mail program good or bad?	Outlook good.
Will my mother come home with some pet pastry goodness?	Don't count on it.

*Widely available at all pet and toy stores.

swing, nothing was going to stop her from hitting that ball. Nothing that is, until IT happened.

"Pfffft.

"Pffft.

"Pfft."

A look of puzzlement came over everyone's face.

Had someone blown a kazoo or sat on a duck?

No. My mother had just farted.

In public.

In front of all her friends.

The hills had momentarily been alive with the sound of music, and now they were filled with the sound of laughter.

My mother turned fifty shades of red, and rightfully so. Looking for comfort she made her way over to me.

I just walked away.

You know what they say, "You reek what you sow."

Part Two
Georgia on My Mind

CHAPTER 15

We're Movin' On Up

It had taken me seven years to get to a place where I finally had the four F's: family, friends, fun, and food. Although I didn't let on, I knew I couldn't ask for a better situation. That, however, was about to change in the blink of an eye.

It was a seemingly ordinary evening until the garage door ground open and my father appeared in the doorway more quickly than usual, looking a bit disheveled. "Well, they made it official today. They're going to relocate our offices to Atlanta."

This possibility had been discussed around the kitchen table for the past few months, but I never took the conversations seriously. Their discussions never led to anything concrete. I mean, how long had they been talking about putting up an arbor for the walkway? Or buying end tables for the bedroom? Or buying food for the fridge? How was I to know they meant business this time?

"So what do we do now?" my mother asked.

"Let's get out a piece of paper and write down the positives and the negatives again."

I looked over their shoulders as they quickly scribbled down their thoughts:

Advantages: Income from a job, a new adventure, can

always come back home if things don't work out, better weather.

Disadvantages: Leaving behind family, friends, and memories.

Nice list, but you may note, as did I, there was nothing on that sheet of paper about me. Had I been responsible for deciding on our destiny the list would have looked something like this:

Advantages: Staying with my food and affection source.

Disadvantages: Losing a forever wild backyard, losing leadership position in the neighborhood pack, no snow, no more romps with friends.

My parents never considered the vast amount of land in our backyard I'd be giving up or the clear alpha dog stature I had achieved in the neighborhood. Nor was the fact considered what effect the sultry Southern weather would have on an extremely hairy dog. Nope, none of that mattered. This decision was all about them.

After a few days of long and intense discussions they made their decision. Much like General Sherman many years prior, the family was headed to Atlanta.

Hopefully they wouldn't burn the place down, too.

After a house-hunting trip, my mother returned home and sat me down on the bed. I sensed she was looking to break some bad news.

"Bo, I don't want you to be disappointed when we get to Georgia, so I'm going to tell this to you straight.

"The houses are nothing like what we saw in *Gone With the Wind* the other night."

Yes, she had gone out to the video store and rented the movie prior to going house hunting with my father in Georgia. I tell no lies.

"There aren't any large Southern mansions, homes with wraparound porches, or cute cottages.

"At least not in our price range, anyway. I just didn't want you to be disappointed when we got there."

I knew that the only disappointed party was my mother. She'd had her heart set on living in a historic southern-style home.

"But I do have good news! We put an offer in on a home. It's a nice house, and you'll be happy to know it has a fenced-in backyard!"

The average dog wouldn't pick up on the consequences of that last statement, but I'm not average. You see, a fenced-in backyard means owners don't feel the need to walk you every day. It lets them off their guilt trip by letting you run "free." The good news is they think you're no freer than a goldfish in a bowl, when in reality you're as free as a mime stuck in a box. Think about it.

The few months of transition saw my father come and go, mostly go, as we prepared the house for sale and ultimately for another family to live in.

My mother boxed up favorite items, strangers showed up to look at the house at all hours of the day, and I had to endure my father's absence, though it was cutting into my exercise time. I wished things could go back to the way they were.

My mother was stressed and my only confidant was Moose. I sure hoped this move was going to be worth it.

My father came home one last time and synchronized with the large moving trucks that hauled our stuff away. He had made the decision to drive the family to our new home. I would have preferred flying, but my parents had various concerns over having me take the friendly skies to Georgia.

I didn't see what the problem was. I wasn't afraid to fly, plus if I was lucky I'd find myself a member of the Mile High Treat Club. You always heard dogs bragging about their membership, you just never believed it.

After a two-day drive, accompanied by Moose's nonstop meowing, we arrived at our new home. The house was nice, certainly much larger than the one we had occupied in New York, plus it had the front porch my mother had always coveted.

Any dog will tell you though, "The front yard is for show, but the backyard is really why you put down the dough."

. I wasn't disappointed. It was a nice size backyard and, as advertised, it was fully fenced in. I noted the architect had made one large mistake in the design of the fence. It was made of wood. Delectable, chewable, tender wood. If I could keep from pigging out on it, I'd be able to partake in it for years to come. And, although word had it that the Georgia clay was tough to dig, I found it to be quite workable under my paws.

This would do. This would do very nicely.

Despite my excitement, we were not allowed to explore the house that first evening. In their infinite wisdom, my parents had scheduled to have the hardwood floors refinished, and they had yet to dry. Since our furniture was also in transit, we slept on the carpeted floor of the finished basement, surrounded by various pillows and blankets.

My father slept with his arm around my mother, who slept with her arm around me, and I slept with my paw around Moose.

The family was in tact, and ready for a new set of adventures.

CHAPTER 16

Enema of the State

The laid-back lifestyle I observed in the suburbs of Atlanta was a welcome change. Dogs barked in a slow drawl, squirrels seemed to jog instead of sprint, and the creeks in the area all tasted like sweet tea. This was the South of Robert E. Lee, Martin Luther King Jr., and Boss Hogg. I vowed to enjoy all of it.

It wasn't long, however, before the excitement of the move and living in a new region of the country wore off. The mundane daily activities took hold and the entire family settled into the roles we had become accustomed to in New York. My father was off to work early in the morning and didn't come home until late at night. My mother dabbled in the antiques business, opening her own booth at the local consignment shop before closing it and looking for her next opportunity. I spent my time figuring out the best way to get on the other side of the fence to run free in the neighborhood.

My sister Moose settled into a routine, too, although hers was a bit different from the rest of the family's. For some reason the Southern lifestyle wasn't conducive to her digestive system. Her activity centered on pooping, or I should say lack of pooping. Ever since our arrival in the Peach State, she struggled with constipation issues. She'd squat in her litter box, her face getting red as she tried to push a kitty snicker through the keyhole, but the only thing she had to show for it was an increased carbon footprint. Although my parents' attempts to minimize these occurrences were wide and varied, inevitably Moose would bind up like an eighty-year-old man on a strict meat and cheese diet.

So I wasn't surprised when my mother proclaimed, "The cat's clogged again!"

"Are you sure?" my father replied.

"Oh, I'm sure," she said. Then, with resignation in her voice, she continued, "I'll call the vet and get her over there today."

Countless times my parents had taken her to the vet for this with the subsequent diagnosis and treatment always the same. Moose was as clogged as a twenty-year-old Kojak's shower drain and would need to receive an enema. Once flushed, Moose would be merrily sent on her way home, only to start the process of getting clogged all over again.

This time would be different.

My mother called the veterinarian's office to make the appointment; however, they were too busy to see her that day. Even though my mother expressed concern over Moose's condition, she made no headway in garnering the coveted appointment. Not one to take no, she escalated the issue, insisting on speaking with one of the veterinarians or technicians on duty. My mother took a brief moment to put on the speakerphone while grabbing a pencil, just in case she needed to write down any pertinent information.

I sat in the corner of the kitchen, with ears cocked forward, curious to see how she'd handle this.

Soon, the sound of a female tech's voice echoed through the room, "Can I help you?"

"Yes. This is Moose's mother. I really need to get her in there today."

"Is she having constipation issues again?" This tech had encountered Moose before.

"Oh, yes. She's clogged and needs another enema."

"I'm really sorry, but we're fully booked. We've had several emergencies today that have backed up everything. We can do it tomorrow."

"I really think Moose needs help today," my mother said, trying to push her agenda.

"I'm sorry but we can't see her today."

"I don't think you understand. She really needs help today."

"I understand. Let me ask you, do you have a turkey baster?" she asked.

My mother was momentarily confused. "A what?"

"A turkey baster. You know, what you use to baste a turkey around Thanksgiving time."

"I don't have a baster. I don't really cook."

"Oh. Really? Well, uhhm, you can call the Butterball hotline. They can tell you where to find one."

"Is that necessary? I'd really just like to make an appointment."

"I'm sorry we're booked full. Since you don't have a baster, do you have any other type of syringes around the house?"

"Well, my husband just had a root canal. He has one of those small syringes that he uses to shoot all the food out of the holes where his teeth used to be."

"That will work perfectly. Do you have Dove liquid soap?"

"I have Ivory liquid soap."

"No, that's too harsh. You need Dove."

"I may have some around here somewhere."

"Great. Mix the Dove with warm water and fill up the syringe. Then, lift your cat's tail and stick it in her butt. Squeeze the syringe so that you release all the liquid inside. That's all there is to it."

"I don't want the recipe! I just want to make an appointment."

"I'm sorry but we just don't have any openings for today."

"I don't know if I can do that."

"It's really not that bad to do, honey. Just remember, you may have to do it again later in the day if she's still clogged, but the second time is a lot easier than the first."

"Are you sure I can't bring her in?"

"I'm sorry but we just don't have a moment to spare today."

"You've given me no choice. I'll give it a try."

I was stunned that my mother would actually agree to try this. This is a woman who blushes at the sight of a Tootsie Roll. Now she was going to give Moose an enema?

There's no way she's pulling this off.

I was on my mother's heels as she ran upstairs to get my father's root canal syringe. I followed her down into the kitchen where she scoured the pantry. There it was, a nice white container of Dove. She mixed the Dove with some warm water and filled the syringe. I couldn't believe it . . . she was going to do the dirty deed!

A performance like this was going to move her up a few spots on my hero chart, right behind Spuds MacKenzie.

But, then . . .

"Honey, I need you!" she innocently yelled to my father from the kitchen.

"Sure, what do you need?" he responded as he walked into the room.

"You need to give the cat an enema."

"A what?"

"An enema. Moose is clogged again and the vet is all booked up today."

"Uhmm, I don't think so. If anybody is going to do it, it's you. Remember, it was *your* idea to get a cat."

"C'mon, she's in pain and needs our help. *Our* help. I'll hold her. You just have to put this in her pooper and squeeze. It's easy. That's what the lady at the vet said."

"I don't think I can do that."

"Stop being a baby. It's not that hard to do."

"It's kinda gross. Plus, I don't know the first thing about giving an enema. It's not like I've ever even gotten an enema, let alone given one. Speaking of which, you know those coffee enemas? Do you think they use Starbucks-type coffee or the low end stuff when they do one of those?"

"Stop changing the subject."

"No, seriously. Do you think Juan Valdez knows what's happening with the coffee beans he's picking?"

"Juan Valdez would help his wife give the cat an enema. Oh, just man up. Isn't that what your friends would say?"

Going after his manliness was a low blow, but it worked its magic. He knew there wasn't any getting out of this, so my father reluctantly submitted to my mother's desire and agreed to give Moose the enema.

With syringe in hand, my parents slowly opened the door to the laundry room where poor, pathetic Moose was just lying there, looking wiped out.

My mother grabbed Moose from the front while my father got the raw end of the deal. Moose realized what they were planning to do and was having none of it. It was bad enough having trained professionals administer her enemas, but to have two bungling vets in training was too much. With her last ounce of energy, Moose curled her tush into her body like a lobster pulling in its tail. It didn't work. My father pried her open like a clam shell, and holding his breath, inserted the small syringe—the syringe that had been designed for his mouth—into Moose's behind.

He shut his eyes, turned his head, and pushed the plunger on the syringe. Moose let out a sound that could only be interpreted as, "You bastards. I'm glad I pissed on your love seat!" My father quickly pulled out the torture device, happy the ordeal was over.

Had the enema been this easy I would hardly consider it worthy of mention, but when my father withdrew the syringe, a stream of chocolate water squirted out right after it. The old man was too slow to miss the oncoming surge and was hit flush in the face with it. The stream was not unlike the stream of water that comes from water pistols at the county fair.

"*Aaaahhhhhhhhh!!*" screamed the six-foot, two-hundred-pound human I call my father.

Dropping the syringe, he ran to the sink and feverishly doused his face with water.

My mother, keeping a safe distance from the mayhem, said, "Eeewwwweee."

After regaining his composure and cleaning his face for the tenth time, my father checked on Moose. She wasn't doing any better.

My mother said, "I hate to tell you this, but you need to do it again. And be careful, it's going to come back at you."

This time my father was ready, and smarter. Making his job easier was that Moose had no fight left. My mother grabbed Moose's head; he grabbed her rear. In went the syringe, the plunger was depressed, and my father pulled it out. He jerked his head to the side, away from Willy Wonka's stream of chocolate just in time. Success! Sure there was crap on the washer, the floor, the wall, Moose, and my father's shirt but this time it didn't hit anybody in the face. Sometimes you have to redefine the meaning of success so you can attain it.

Throughout the afternoon a few more enemas were successfully administered. Moose finally moved her bowels that day; and in a land far, far away so did Juan Valdez.

CHAPTER 17

Madge of Honor

Some years are like long walks in the park: fun, easy, and exhilarating. Other years are like baths: uncomfortable, emotionally draining, and a true test of wills. Our family was about to have one huge bath. Unfortunately the water contained no bubbles and the tub's surroundings were void of any bacon-scented candles.

"I had an accident with your truck!"

My mother had just returned from the store where she'd been tasked to get me a box of beef-flavored chewys. I could tell by the sound of her voice she was a little shaken; I was shaken, too. Had she forgotten my treats?

My father came running. "What? Are you okay? What happened?"

"I got rear-ended at a traffic light. Luckily the girl who hit me wasn't going fast, but my back and chest hurt."

"Do you need to go to the doctor?"

"No, I'll be all right. I'm just sore."

It seems humans don't like going to the vet any more than canines do.

It took several weeks before my mother was herself again and I was allowed to jump on her in bed without being yelled at. The happy, good old days had returned.

Days later she left for her annual pilgrimage home to visit

her parents. Upon her return she brought back gifts and a new discomfort in her arm. It was a shooting pain down her limb accompanied by a stabbing sensation in her chest. Presumably this was all due to her lifting heavy luggage.

Day by day, she struggled with the pain as her spirit slowly diminished.

Over the course of several months she visited numerous doctors, each of whom insisted she had pulled a muscle in her arm, and as far as the stabbing pain she felt in her chest, that was all in her head.

My mother never slept through the night anymore, so neither did I.

She wasn't the same. There were no more unplanned car rides to the countryside, walks in the woods, or even trips to the pet store. No, my mother would just lie on the couch, nursing the constant pain she felt, each and every day.

This affected my father, too. Although he wasn't around during the day to experience it, he saw its effects in the evening and on the weekends. His wife rarely smiled and turned emotionally inward rather than being the open, sharing human being he had been accustomed to. Plus he could do no right. Anything he touched was met with disapproval from my mother, whether he deserved it or not. Mostly not.

On weekends we were all together in a room physically, but emotionally, we were lost in our own thoughts. It was as if a rain cloud hung over each of our heads.

It's true what they say, if you don't have a healthy owner, you don't have anything.

My mother went to physical therapy, endured cortisone shots, and downed anti-inflammatory cocktails all to no avail. It wasn't until my father discovered a lump the size of a softball on her back that the doctors finally took her seriously.

Ten Things I've Had in My Mouth

The barrel of a gun

A Ginsu knife

Alvin the chipmunk

Pinecones

The windowsill

Rocky the squirrel

Kitty crap

Silver coins—I don't bother with copper ones

Rubik's Cube (solved it, too)

Moose's head

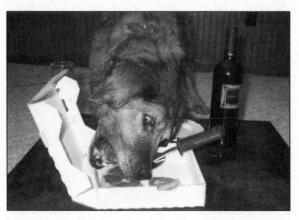

I almost forgot to add pizza and wine to the list.

My parents thought I was oblivious to what was happening around me, that I was still the happy-go-lucky dog I always was. Hadn't they noticed I spent twenty-four hours a day moping around the house with this woman? Most times I knew before she did what she would do next. Granted if I said, "She's going to go to the bathroom, grab a tissue, and blow her nose," I had an 80 percent chance of being right.

So by the time the diagnosis came back, I already knew it wasn't good. Dogs are good at sniffing it out. It was the big C, a cancerous tumor that had been growing inside her chest all this time. No one in the house is allowed to call it that, though. My mother will only let it be called "Madge" since it sounds less frightening.

Over the next few days, my parents came and went from various doctor appointments. During their time at home, we all sat around trying to enjoy each other's company, but that dark cloud still hung over us. Things just weren't the same.

A week after the diagnosis, my mother and father packed up her pajamas and left the house for the hospital.

When the door slammed shut, I was alone and scared. I ran upstairs and lay on my mother's side of the bed, taking in her smell. I didn't want to let her go.

I lay there for hours. After it turned dark, I listened for their car to make its way into the driveway. It didn't come until well past midnight.

I ran to the door and greeted them. My father looked tired, a few years older than when he had left. I waited for my mother to come through the door, but she never did. I had suspected as much.

In bed, I snuggled up tight to my father and fell asleep. No sooner had my eyes closed than the alarm woke us up.

He was up, much earlier than his normal routine, hurriedly fed me, and left the house. I was alone again.

During lunch, a neighbor stopped by to let me out and to feed me. After their fifteen minute stop-by, I was alone with my thoughts again.

Like in the movie *Groundhog Day*, this record repeated itself over the next few days. The only difference was that my father's appearance was deteriorating by the day. I wished he'd fill me in on what was happening.

My life was in disarray. It was the longest I'd ever been apart from my mother, and I hardly saw my father.

Several days later, my father came home late at night with someone in tow. I smelled them before they walked through the door. The visitor's scent was familiar—and even held a faint whiff of my mother. But it was my grandmother— instead. From her big, and I mean big, suitcase, I assumed her stay would not be a short one. The bag was large enough to hide Sasquatch and a friend, should they ever need to travel from Maine to California in the belly of a plane. My father struggled to get it up the stairs.

Anxiety rushed through my body. He hadn't swapped out my mother for the older model, had he? If so, I was getting a raw deal. I loved my mother, even with all her quirks. Didn't he know how long it took me to train her?

But I have to tell you, I was happy to have some company. I know, I was desperate.

Even though it was late, both of them settled in on the couch. I listened intently in hopes of determining the whereabouts of my beloved mother.

"The doctor said the surgery was successful," my father said as he took a deep breath. He had a worried look on his face, and his tone didn't inspire confidence that he actually believed what the surgeon had told him. He continued. "He did say, though, that it's an aggressive tumor and because he wasn't able to get a positive margin around all of it she'll need to follow up with radiation treatments once she's up to it."

"Is she always in that much pain?" my grandmother asked. They had stopped by the hospital on the way home from the airport.

"Oh, yeah. She's pretty uncomfortable, even with the pain-killers they're giving her. The doctor said he had to cut out some nerves and muscle, so it's going to be a long time recovering."

"I just don't understand why it took this long for the doctors to figure it out."

"Me, either. I guess it's a matter of finding the right one. Once Dr. Blanc took a look at her, he scheduled the surgery immediately. We'll never know if things would have been different if she got diagnosed earlier."

"Well, at least it's out now and we can focus on getting her healthy again."

"Let's hope it doesn't return. Anyway, we better get to bed. I have to get up early so I can go to the hospital in the morning."

"I hope you don't mind, but I'm not real good in hospitals. I'll just stay here and clean."

I raised my paw and volunteered, "Hey, I'll go!"

"Bo, be quiet!" my father quipped before continuing. "It's no problem at all. I think your visit today did a lot to lift her spirits. Besides, if you stay here I don't have to worry about the neighbor having to come over to feed Bo. He could use the company, too."

That came out way too quick and smooth. I think he was happy to leave her home with me! I wanted to see my mother! Why do I always get the short end of the throwing stick?

Early the following morning, my father got up and left

the house. It was just me and the grandmother. She rose about eleven o'clock by my calculation and made her cup of coffee. She gave me some dry food. I didn't eat it. She gave me some lunch meat. I ate that.

Maybe this situation wasn't so bad after all.

She spent the rest of the day running up and down the stairs, cleaning and scrubbing every exposed surface in the house. Frankly, I didn't realize the filth I had been living in. If I had a white glove for my paw, I could have rubbed it on the floor, in the corner, and not come up with a speck of dust. She was good. She was a cleaning machine.

At about 10:00 in the evening the phone rang and she picked up. On the other end was my father.

"How's she doing?" she asked.

After listening to my father's report she said, "I guess it's good she's heavily medicated. The less she remembers of this, the better."

A few more moments of silence on our end were followed with, "Well that's good to hear. Hey, did you know we don't have any milk? I was wondering if you could stop by the store on the way back and pick some up?

"You can? That's great. Make sure it's skim milk, it's better for you. Thanks and tell my daughter I love her."

Well past midnight, my father walked through the door, milk in hand. Skim milk rather than the creamy whole milk the family thrived on.

I waited for him to arrive every night, and although we only had six hours together, I soaked in every minute of it. To his credit he always brought me home something special: the smell of my mother. She was on his hands, face, and clothes. I lay in bed with him sniffing him up and down. To the average dog, she may have smelled a little "gamey," but to this love-starved mutt, she smelled as sweet as the oriental lilies she so adores.

Each day the reports on my mother's health got better . . . less painkillers, more awareness. Each day my father got instructions on what to bring home: egg beaters instead of eggs, double ply toilet paper instead of single ply, low-fat cream cheese instead of the real stuff. I even put in a request for a low-fat grandmother instead of the regular one, but he never brought that home.

One morning, my father left the house with a tone of excitement in his voice and a bounce in his step. I kept my paws crossed as to what it could be, but I didn't want to get my hopes up.

After I had eaten my lunch, I heard the familiar sound of our car pull into the driveway. I ran to the window to see my father get out, walk around the car, and help my mother out the other side. She was home! She was home!

I jumped up and down, circling my grandmother.

I watched as my mother gingerly walked to the door. I couldn't wait to greet her, but was never given the chance. Instead, my grandmother grabbed me by my collar and showed me the door—the back door, into the yard.

I yelled to be let in.

Eventually my grandmother let me in and I sprinted from room to room, sniffing out my mother. When I finally discovered the one she was in, the door was closed, but I could hear voices murmuring on the other side. I scratched at the door to let my mother know I was there.

Some time later, my father squeezed out of the door, careful not to let me in. He grabbed my leash and secured it on my collar. Once he had me under his control, he led me into the master bedroom where my mother lay.

She was pale and her voice was weak, but her excitement shone through.

I tried to jump on the bed and lay a big wet kiss on her,

but my father wouldn't let me. Instead, he escorted me around to her side of the bed, where she petted me.

Oooohhh that felt so good and I was ecstatic to smell her up close and personal. She was back!

Then my mother said, "You can let him up. I think it will be okay."

My father unleashed me and I jumped up on the bed, jostling my mother from side to side. This would have been all right if she didn't have sixty staples holding her back together, but she did. My mother screamed in pain and my father screamed in anger. I was unceremoniously tossed from the room.

One transgression and I was banned! Apparently they had not taken notice that I had the highest-rated* bedside manner this side of the Chattahoochee River. Whether I liked it or not I was relegated to waiting outside of the room where I guarded the door and access to my beloved mother.

That evening while I circled to make my bed outside my mother's door, I heard her call to me, "Bo, Bo, I missed you."

I barked gently, "I missed you, too," as a joyful tear rolled down my cheek.

We had a long road ahead of us, but at least the family was together again.

---

*Source: Pugsy Health Worker's Customer Satisfaction Survey—Southeast Region.

CHAPTER 18

Woody and the Gun

For the first week after my mother's return from the hospital, I noticed my father was also made to sleep on the floor at night. Apparently he couldn't be trusted on the bed, either. I felt a little better about my banishment from the room.

She was still in a lot of pain, and hopped up on plenty of medication. Fortunately the drugs allowed her to sleep a lot, and in the periods she wasn't, my grandmother or father would bring her soup and sandwiches to eat.

All in all we remained very quiet, lest we disturb her recovery. Things were going well—until Woody showed up.

When she had been home for two days, my mother started complaining about a strange knocking sound on the bedroom wall. My mother said she thought she was going crazy, that something was sending Morse code messages from the inside of her skull. I thought it was probably the drugs talking.

Then, I heard it, too. Being a creature of the wild I recognized the sound; it was a woodpecker. Given plenty of time to analyze the beat of the sound, I was able to discern a repeating cadence. Maybe it was a message of great importance? I didn't have time to find out, but maybe someone reading this does. The exact pattern, etched in my mind, was

-... . / ... ..- .-. . /--- / -.. .-. .. -. -.- / -.-- --- ..- .-. /
--- ...- .- .-..-.. -. .

Three days of incessant pounding later, and my mother was forced to double up on her painkillers. The constant hammering was torture, pure and simple. The only reprieve she got was when she left the house to visit the doctor's office. I don't know which was the worse of the two. Even I was ready to put a bullet through my head. Suddenly, a thought occurred to me.

"Wait a minute," I pondered, "why should I put a bullet in my head when I can just shoot Woody in the brain instead?" After all, my mother deserved to recover in peace, didn't she?

I scoured the house for a gun I could use, only to find out that my parents may be pacifists, or worse, anti-gun liberals. We lived in a Georgia suburb where it was illegal *not* to have a gun in your house. I began to wonder whether the old man knew his friends probably called him "Cupcake" behind his back.

Without access to a firearm, I was left to my own devices to fix the situation, so I started to yell at Woody to quiet down. This didn't present a problem when my parents were out, but when they returned and put my mother back in bed, it turned into a bone of contention.

I was just trying to reason with the woodpecker, telling him we had a sick lady in the house and to just move it along, you know, maybe next door to the preacher's house. When he wouldn't listen, I continued to make my case, which unfortunately sounds a lot like barking to my owners. The next thing I knew everyone was yelling at me! Hey, I was just trying to fix this situation. The easy answer to the family's problem was simple. Buy a gun; shoot the bird.

Hello? McFly? Anybody home?

The relentless pecking continued as my mother tried to recover in the room directly on the other side of Woody's wall. Even the drugs she was taking weren't able to induce a deep enough sleep to keep the sound from penetrating her mind.

Every time Woody started his routine, my mother would place a phone call to my father's office, conveniently located in the basement, to plead, "Honey, please make him stop. He's driving me crazy. I can't get any rest."

"I'm trying. I 'shoo' him away when I see him, but he keeps coming back. I even threw an apple at him."

"You missed him, didn't you?"

"Yeah, but it was close."

Contradicting her stance on all living things, outside of spiders, she suggested, "Can't you just shoot him?"

Somebody else maybe, but not my father. He couldn't kill time if he had to.

"I just can't do that, honey," was his response.

Even his mother-in-law chimed in, "That bird is awful. Somebody should shoot it."

No one did. Woody continued to have his pecking rights intact.

My mother slowly got better. A week of staying in bed, she started venturing downstairs to sit for minutes at a time. This was my first real chance to rub up against her and feel her physical presence. She was looking better, and her attitude was positive, too. It was a welcome change.

One night, I walked in as my father was helping her put on a nightshirt. Briefly exposed was her bare back, now riddled with staples. It looked as if a Great White had bitten her along her back. I now understood why it was taking her so long to recover.

Several weeks after my mother's return, her mother packed up her belongings and headed home. The house was clean, the food in the fridge healthy, and most important her daughter wasn't in bed all day anymore, able to get up, and even shower by herself.

Although she would leave the family, Woody decided to stay.

My parents introduced a new routine into our lives, that being the daily ride to the radiation treatment center. Inexplicably, I was not welcome to join them on these trips. How rude.

But my father tells me what goes on.

"It's a lot like the vet's. You do a lot of waiting. Eventually they come to get your mother. And I sit there and wait for her.

"Because most patients require weeks of treatments, most will schedule to come the same time every day. You see the same folks over and over again. Well, there's this one older gentleman that I struck up a conversation with and I tell him about Woody."

At this point I thanked my lucky stars I wasn't invited along on these trips. Bringing up Woody is only going to make us look bad.

He continued his story. "So, Bo, this older gentleman knows what to do about him! He says, *'First thing . . . make sure ya don't got no bugs infestin' the house. Them woodpeckers love bugs.'*

"Then he continues on and says, *'Once ya know it ain't that, then what ya need to do, and this is gonna sound crazy, but it works, is hang tin foil over the area he's pecking at.'*

"Tin foil? Can you imagine that, Bo?"

No I couldn't. Besides, I knew my father would have difficulty giving up all that material for his hats.

"So buddy, the man goes on to tell me other ways to get Woody to stop banging away at the house. *'Well I heard ya can hang a black garbage bag over the hole, too. If you're wantin' to do that. Yessiree lots a ways to stop 'em. Ya can also paint the area he's chippin' at, but ya need to mix some a that there cayenne pepper into the paint. That way, he gets himself a snoot full a heat. Trust me; he ain't gonna like that one bit.'"*

This guy sounded like a bit of a psycho to me, but my father was thoroughly intrigued.

"And then he says, *'Of course ya could just shoot 'em instead.'"*

Okay, now he sounds normal.

Shaking his head, my father finished with, "I just don't understand why everybody wants to shoot Woody."

The rides to radiation continued as my father put the old man's advice into action. He made an appointment with the pest control company, and days later, after the house was deemed relatively pest-free, my father hung a large black garbage bag directly over the portion of the house on which Woody had been pounding away.

It didn't look pretty, and it may have broken a few home owner association covenants, but amazingly it stopped Woody from his pecking ways. The only issue now was how to get the neighbors to stop laughing at this house, this family, and by extension me. I think I'm in hell. No really.

At least I could rest in peace during the days now. My mother appreciated the silence, too, even if it did come a little late.

Woody visited us every year for the next five years, pecking away at the exact spot each time. He was a reminder of a difficult time, but also a symbol that things do get better. It wasn't until my father replaced the siding where our feathery friend had excavated a sizable chunk out of the house that Woody moved on.

He never returned; and I'm happy to report, neither did Madge.

CHAPTER 19

The Preacher, the Chipmunk, and Me

I don't care where you live, whether it's in a trailer park, in a middle-class neighborhood, or in an upscale condo community, there's one thing you can't control: your neighbors. Specifically, neighbors of the human persuasion. Sometimes that's good. Most times it's not.

I would say our particular neighborhood wasn't any different from others in America. We had our share of teachers, government workers, and office lemmings. There were the soccer moms, construction workers, and virtual office folks, too. And lest I forget, among this throng of citizenry was a smattering of mental patients.

Take Lou, for instance. He was a portly man in his fifties who asked my father for help numerous times and about all sorts of things. Computer issues? No problem. How about cameras, know anything about them? Of course. And rabbits? Love 'em, especially in a stew.

Soon enough, Lou couldn't get out of bed without asking my father the best way to do it. Lou wasn't interested in learning how to fish, he was happy living across the street from a fully stocked fishery.

One day, Lou called in a panic. He needed my father for

an emergency situation he had on his hands. My father dutifully complied.

I waited by the doorway for his return, and more importantly to hear the reason for the latest 911 call.

When my father returned home a short time later, my mother asked, "What was it this time?"

"Well, he's going on a trip and needed help with his bag."

"That was his emergency? What was wrong with his bag?"

"Nothing."

"Then why did he ask you for help?"

"He needed my help to put the luggage tag on."

I almost choked on the slice of pastrami I was sharing with my mother.

It was clear, somewhere in the state, an institution was missing a patient.

Another member of the neighborhood long-armed shirt brigade was a short, paunchy fellow named Carmichael. There was only one thing Carm loved more than mowing his lawn: mowing it with his shirt off. Don't get me wrong, I go shirtless all the time, so I don't have a problem with it per se, but Carm would come over to the house afterward, invite himself in, and sit down on the living room couch. There's just something wrong about a sweaty human, with wet back hair, leaning against cushions I wasn't even allowed on. Maybe it wouldn't have been so wrong if he'd brought a treat with him once in a while.

Of course we also had the neighbors in full denial as to the devious nature of their teenage kids. Every year, Al and Peg left their teenage kids at home while they set off on a weeklong vacation. The kids would inevitably throw a party with drinking and loud music going on until all hours of the morning. Apparently they didn't get the memo: Bo needs his beauty sleep. I'd be up all night barking at them.

Yet these parents were oblivious to their children's antics. Following one of their trips, I actually overheard the neighbor saying to my mother, "Dawn is just so special. She cleaned the entire house for us while we were gone."

Of course she did. Teenage puke doesn't come out of the carpet by itself, especially if you don't have a dog around to lick it up. I'm still offended I wasn't invited to help tidy up the place.

I could understand this willful blindness to see the best in your family. Heaven knows my parents were afflicted with it, too—otherwise, how could you explain why they loved me? However, I didn't understand why it extended to my neighbor next door, the one they called the Preacher.

The Preacher was a compassionate human being who loved the company of his fellow man and spread the word of God at the local church. His soft-spoken approach, disarming smile, and heartfelt kindness endeared him to all of his friends and followers. He was also kind to animals.

On the surface he passed the sniff test, but after meeting him I couldn't shake the feeling he had a deeper, darker side. Nobody was this good, this perfect.

I watched every day from the living room window that overlooked the back of his house and yard, noting anything out of the ordinary. It wasn't long before my notebook was full and I was certain there were strange goings on in that compound of his.

I noticed squirrels entered his yard but never left, birds soared in but never flew out, and when two rabbits hopped in, only twelve bound out. His backyard was the Bermuda Triangle for the wild life set.

Was I the only one who noticed, or was I being paranoid? I peered out at the Preacher's house contemplating this question when I witnessed a rifle's barrel slowly emerge from the second-story window. A left arm supported the rifle as a right hand took its proper place near the trigger. The standard

Ten Things That Taste Like Chicken

 Chicken

 Johnny Cash

 Frog legs

 Ear wax

 Possum on an open fire

 Rocky Mountain oysters

 Belly lint

 Poulet basquaise

 Squirrel roadkill, over easy

Toe cheese

Kitty food is the other white meat.

wood gunstock, buried in the crook of an old man's arm, partially covered a wool, plaid shirt.

I jerked my head around to alert my parents who were watching TV in the room.

"The killer! I see the killer!" I barked.

"Bo, be quiet."

"Look! Somebody needs to stop him!"

"Quiet!"

I snapped my head back to the action outside my rear window.

He held the gun steady, real steady. He'd done this before. His right index finger moved into position on the trigger head as he reminded himself that "he mustn't pull the trigger, just squeeze it instead." I was sure all snipers thought this.

With one eye closed, he took dead aim at his prey.

"Don't move, Alvin," I envisioned him saying. "Don't move, and you'll be sleeping with Chip and Dale before you know it."

"Run, Alvin, run!" I said through clenched teeth.

A gunshot rang out, followed by the sound of rustling leaves and a sickening thud.

"Noooooo!" I whimpered.

"Bo, quit your whining."

Then an ominous silence spread over the yard. As quickly as the old man had appeared in the window he was gone, and it was as if the grisly scene I'd just witnessed had never happened at all.

I scoured the wooded lot with my eyes, fortunate to see where the chipmunk fell. It was quite the header Alvin took off the limb of that dogwood tree, for if the bullet didn't kill him, the precipitous drop surely did.

I sprang into action, crossing my paws while I whined incessantly, the universal signal for needing to go outside.

My parents quickly acquiesced to my desires by opening the door. I made a beeline to the base of the dogwood. Sure enough, Alvin lay dead at the base of one of my favorite trees, and best of all, easily accessible.

I hovered over him, sniffing his little fuzzy body from head to claw. He looked peaceful, as if he were asleep. One would not have guessed he was dead other than the single blood spot right over his heart. Damn, that Preacher was one hell of a shot.

Being a compassionate canine (a slogan I had just run my 2000 Senate campaign under), I felt the need to give the poor little guy a proper burial. It was the least I could do for a member of the suburban animal kingdom. I decided to bring Alvin into the house while I worked out the funeral arrangements.

"Taps" played in my head as I put my mouth around him and began the jaunt back home. His lifeless body bounced up and down with every step I took. I stopped, for if my parents saw him dangling from my jowls, they'd be sure to bar me from going inside. So, I crammed Alvin deep into my mouth like a hot dog eating champion does to, well, hot dogs.

At the back door, I barked to be let in. It wasn't my normal deep, radio worthy bark, but rather a sheepish, lispy one. It wasn't easy with a chipmunk in my mouth.

My mother opened the door, eyeballing me suspiciously. Had she been watching me? Had she seen me retrieve Alvin? Had she noticed I looked like a chipmunk? I put my head down and pushed past her.

She grabbed my collar to keep me from going any farther than the entrance. Yup, she knew something was up. She always knows, especially when my mouth is closed and there's no sight of my black tongue.

I was carrying something all right, but in my defense it was usually nuts, not gunshot victims.

My mother called my father for reinforcement, and he came running down the stairs.

I pulled my chin in close to my chest as I looked up with my innocent brown eyes.

"What ya got, buddy? You hiding an acorn or something?"

"I don't think so. There's something furry hanging out the side of his mouth," my mother volunteered.

"Is that your fake, stuffed doggie bone?"

"I don't think it's his stuffed bone, either," my mother countered.

My father bent down to see what I had. Eye to eye, he gave me the "Give it!" command.

Who was he kidding, that only works in the movies.

I turned my head as he reached for my snout, and then quickly to the other side as he tried to grab it again. I wasn't giving up Al easy.

"Honey, hold his head while I pry his mouth open." They loved teaming up on me.

My mother moved in and held me tight while the old man forced my mouth open.

Out fell Alvin, as serene as before but this time with drool on his chest.

My mother screamed in horror at the corpse lying in her hallway.

"Bo, what did you do? Bad boy! Why do you have to go out and kill things? Bad Boy!"

My father chimed in, "Bo! You are a bad boy! Bad boy!"

They didn't understand me, but hey, I'm a complex dog.

"Why did you have to kill an innocent chipmunk? If you were going to kill anything, why not kill the woodpecker?"

Uhmm, maybe because I can't climb up the side of a house.

I could see the disappointment in their eyes. But I proudly took the fall. After all, a dog being called a hunter isn't going to hurt his reputation among the pack in the neighborhood. My father swept Alvin into a dustpan and buried him in the garbage can outside. I couldn't help but feel I had let Alvin down.

To this very day, my parents think I killed Alvin. I never had the heart to tell them the truth.

So here it is folks, it really wasn't me that killed the chipmunk. It was the kindly old fellow next door, the one you call the Preacher and the one Alvin calls his killer.

Now when folks move into the neighborhood, it is our house that's pointed out. And they'll say, "Be careful, strange things go on over there."

Of course they do. My parents live there.

CHAPTER 20

Precious Metal

From the day they adopted me, it never occurred to my parents to consider adopting another canine. They figured I was soaking up all the love they could dish out, and any move in getting a new family member would just dilute what I was getting. Besides, look at the disaster that was Moose's adoption. Although a cat was one thing, they reasoned bringing another canine into the family would make me unhappy. A reason, which may surprise you, I did not agree with.

Let me explain my position. We all know that too much of a good thing weakens it. It's like being around the Thanksgiving dinner table. At first you're all excited about the dropped piece of turkey. That first piece tastes awesome, and then you realize there's another one and then another! It's an abundance of turkey meat falling from the sky! The problem is, it's too much, too soon. By the end of the meal, you're scarfing the meat down just to put another turkey notch on your collar, but you don't enjoy it anymore. Then, the next thing you know, you're conked out on the sofa sleeping off a tryptophan-induced coma lasting twelve hours. You're not even awake to beg for a slab of the pumpkin pie.

See? Too much of a good thing.

To truly appreciate it, you have to be wanting at some point. Imagine if you were to receive turkey and pumpkin pie every day, spread out over the year. Not only would you want to get up every morning, but in total, you'd appreciate it a lot more. That's all I'm saying.

And so it is with love. Even with my mother's recent work as a secret shopper, we were always within eyeballing distance of each other. It was 24/7 with her, and 24/2 with my father. I never wanted for love because I always got it, and this diluted its value.

A test of my theory would soon occur, beginning on a beautiful fall Saturday, with temperatures in the high sixties and tree leaves turning to a shock of orange. Put another way, it was a perfect day for my parents to go out and do something fun. Unfortunately, my fuzzy behind was stuck inside the house to sleep the day away.

Their planned destination was an apple fest in north Georgia. To magnify the good time, they asked some friends to come along, check out some crafts, and buy some apples. I'm sure my father asked my mother, "How do you like them apples?" at least fifty times that day. She'd be the first to tell you he can be redundant at times, and idiotic, too.

When my parents got back late that night, they sat me down for a serious conversation.

They didn't need to say a thing. I already knew my mother cheated on me that day with another dog. It was written all over her face, but more enlightening were the smells embedded in her jeans and shirt. She'd had more than a chance encounter, that I was sure. But this is nothing new. All canines are forced to face the consequences of their owners' wandering hands. It's in their genes. I was just lucky not to be owned by a shelter worker or a pet store employee. I couldn't live with the repeated indiscretion that would entail.

"First of all, we love you, Bo," my mother began. "It isn't finalized yet, but we may be adopting a canine sister for you."

I was shocked, hopeful, and joyous. I urged her to continue.

"We were at the apple fest and we were walking around for what seemed to be days, when we spotted an ice cream booth.

"You know how much your father loves ice cream! There was no way we're getting past that stand without stopping. After we got our cones, Mary, you know her as Bandit's mom, suggested we sit down to eat our cold treats right next to the doggie adoption folks!"

My father continued the story. "It's amazing how fate works, Bo. A craving here, a suggestion there, and—boom— you've set the wheels of destiny in motion.

"So after your mother takes two licks of her cone, she decides to take a closer look at the dogs. There was this one midsize puppy that sensed your mother's interest. Immediately the dog does a triple lux with a half twist, ending up on her back. Even the East German shepherd judge gave her a 10 for that move.

"Of course this caught your mother's eye and she began petting her while she lay in a submissive state on her back."

Noticing the curious look on my face, he clarified. "No, Bo, it was the dog in a submissive state on her back, not your mother.

"I know this won't surprise you, but your mother immediately started working me to adopt this dog. I was worried about not giving you enough time and attention if we were to adopt another."

Please, I could use the sleep.

My mother jumped in. "I suggested you could use some canine company. Once I presented your father with this argument, he bent like a wet noodle. Well, not totally, because we ended up making a deal.

"The deal was: if the puppy were still un-adopted in four weeks we would make her the newest addition to the family."

My father stepped in again. "It's a clever move by me, Bo. That pup is so cute she's probably already adopted. We'll call the rescue in a month, but I suspect she'll already be gone."

Why were they toying with my emotions. I may be getting a sister, but probably not. What kind of serious talk is that?

As shrewd as my father was, my mother was shrewder. She called the rescue group every other day checking on the status of her precious girl. Each night she'd tell my father how great it would be to add the dog to the pack. After two weeks, she'd worn him down enough to get him to agree. We soon found ourselves on the way to Tennessee to pick up, and hopefully bond with, our new family member.

Upon our arrival, my initial impression of my new sister was that she wasn't so much cute like my mother said, but rather odd looking. She looked like a midget deer, I mean, little deer. She was all legs and had a long body and a pointy-nosed head.

Her name was Copper and she was a Rhodesian ridgeback, a breed famous for hunting lions in Africa. That sounds like a majestic and exciting background, but even with this lineage, nobody wanted her. She was found as a stray on Copper Mountain, or so the story goes, and was most likely dumped there because she didn't have the ridgeback the breed is coveted for. In my book, that makes her a ridge-less Rhodesian ridgeback, a misfit just like the rest of us.

Welcome to the island.

My father led me out of the car, with leash fully secured, and allowed me to approach her. Rather than stand there for the canine smelling tango, she threw herself down on the ground and rolled on her back.

She was just my type, submissive.

I looked up at my parents and gave them the nod. This one will do. We got into the car for the long journey home. So what does Copper do among a total group of strangers? She lies down and falls right to sleep. What a trusting soul, and a lucky one at that. What if we had been killers, or worse, owners of a Chinese restaurant?

When we arrived home later that evening, I played the proper host and showed Copper around. I walked the fence line with her, pointing out the vulnerable spots for future reference. I showed her where to do her business and which trees the squirrels liked to walk down on. I directed her attention to where our neighborhood dogs liked to meet up in the morning, and which ones to be careful of.

That first evening she slept in the crate next to my bed. You know, it's the big one I share with my parents. That night she let loose with the first of what has now been counted in the tens of thousands—a fart.

My kid canine sister, the new kid on the block, loved to pass gas, a fact oddly left out on all the application forms. After having spent several evenings with her, I'd say only unregulated Chinese steel factories rival the amount of pollution she pushed into the air. It had a broccoli-like smell to it, which I kind of liked but my parents weren't fans of. Too bad for them since, by the time they realized this was "normal", she was already well ensconced in our family.

The other detail never mentioned before her adoption was that Copper loves licking—people, places, and things. She experiences the world through her tongue instead of her nose. Being part of the hound family, you'd think she'd have some self-respect and use the skills given her.

What a tragedy; that's like choosing to be Forrest Gump when you're really Einstein.

Copper suffered from a host of other issues: a handful of allergies, chronic ear infections, and snores that were worse than the old man's. And just my luck, she didn't know how to play if her life depended on it. How this train wreck of a dog was signed up to tame lions in the Serengeti is one of those jokes God is constantly playing on us.

That first night, Copper showed she was grateful for my hospitality by licking my face and ears. It was at that point I realized we were going to have a great life together. She was cute, smart, and down to earth. Plus, she accepted her role as number two on the doggie totem pole with grace and charm. What more could a brother want? Her long tongue, dripping with saliva, keeps me from having to shower every day, which is nice. In addition, she'll defer to me when it comes to supper although once I leave the bowl it's all fair game.

She's also good about warming up the bed in the winter. She's slow on the bark but quick on the howl, and when she isn't sleeping her twenty plus hours a day, she's a great companion to have.

And in the end, my theory turned out to be right.

My parents' love, that I now shared with Copper, surpassed the love that had come before.

CHAPTER 21

The Hostess with the Mostess

"Honey, what should I do? You know I'm only a one-trick pony!" my mother pleaded, hoping that my father would pull an answer out of his well-worn hat.

After thinking for a long moment he finally blurted out, "You'll just have to come up with something else to make, that's all."

Then, to soften the blow, he offered, "If it sucks, we'll tell people I made it."

It was the holidays and my parents had been invited to two parties, both of which asked the attendees to bring a dish. A relatively large percentage of the partygoers would be going to both, and my mother was concerned about bringing the same dish. That, coupled with her one-trick pony wardrobe, had her in a tizzy.

"I can make the Chocolate Mousse for the first party, but what about the second one?" she thought out loud.

"What about that fruit dip you told me about? You said it tasted great at Bunco."

"Hey, that's not a bad idea. I can make that! Honey, you're a genius," she said as the weight of the world lifted from her shoulders.

The first party, and dish, went off without a hitch. But that was expected.

The night of the second party she went to make her dip, finding she only had no-fat sour cream instead of the real stuff. She used it anyway.

After she asked my father to taste-test her concoction, my father obliged. "That's really good."

"Are you sure you like it? I'm not sure."

"No, it's tasty." He was lying. I could tell by the tone of his voice and his scrunched up face.

The old man knew his wife. I knew her, too. If he would have told her the truth, he'd be sent out to buy the real ingredients. It was better to lie.

He gave me the bowl to lick. He was right, it sucked.

At the party, nobody ate any of it. At the end of the party, my mother didn't even try to get her dish back. She didn't want anyone to know she made it.

She was right not to let on.

This was just one episode in a string of epic fails. She once made Hamburger Helper for dinner only to be surprised there wasn't any hamburger in it. Her gingerbread men, which bore an uncanny resemblance to the Chucky character from the horror movies, scared kids and adults alike. And of course the one dinner party she'd had in years was ruined when she burned the salmon.

"You got any tartar sauce?" isn't what you want your guests asking.

When my mother told her sister of the latest humiliation, it was agreed that a few cooking lessons were in order, and Chef Catcollector made arrangements for a visit.

This was good news. As you know, we didn't get many visitors when we were in New York, and we got less of them once we moved to Georgia. As the visit drew near, my parents rejoiced, knowing the pack members they left behind still loved them.

My mood improved when I discovered that the Catcollectors were bringing along their new canine family member, AJ.

Surely, this was the missing ingredient that would make it a great visit.

You may recall that once upon a time, Marcy had a penchant for cats. But as the years went by, she and her husband began to realize the folly of their small-minded ways. Sensing they were missing out on something very special, they decided to take action and adopt a canine of their very own. The end result was AJ, an Australian shepherd mix that became their prized possession, the light of their lives, and my much-anticipated house guest.

Copper and I waited anxiously inside as the Dodge Caravan holding our coveted visitors lurched into our driveway. The vehicle was jam packed with stuff . . . lots of stuff . . . for our guests were also antique nuts and had made numerous stops on the nineteen-hour trip to Atlanta. I was immediately reminded of *Beverly Hillbillies*. The only thing missing was Grandma Clampett on top.

As if on cue, the van backfired in the driveway.

When the door to the house opened, AJ sprinted in, full of puppy joy. Copper, never having graduated from etiquette school, immediately attacked our guest. A flurry of activity followed as humans tried to separate the two canines. My mother and Aunt Catcollector screamed at Copper to stop, but I egged her on. Hey, I like a little excitement every now and then—and better Copper than me. The mayhem finally ended when my father pried Copper away from a visibly shaken AJ. What an entrance; this was going to be a fun two weeks of roughhousing!!

When I took Copper to the side to find out what had provoked her, she told me she didn't like strange "pretty boys" coming into her house like they owned it. It was a good thing she didn't have problems with familiar ones.

"What is wrong with your dog? Can't you control her?" Aunt Marcy asked.

"Well, Copper is very good with people, but with other dogs we have to socialize her a bit more," was all my father could come up with. As he spoke, he picked up the tufts of fur ripped from AJ's head and offered them to our guests.

Taking the fur, Uncle Catcollector chimed in, "Socialize her? She just Rodney King'd my dog!"

"In all fairness, AJ did come running into Copper's territory without warning. We just need to make sure to keep an eye on them," my mother said in order to de-escalate the situation.

"As long as you keep an eye on your vicious dog, I'll keep an eye on poor AJ," my aunt retorted.

From that point on, the humans in charge watched all canine interactions as closely as a dog eyeballing a plate of leftovers, and I began to fear our fun with AJ would end right there. On the brighter side, we did get to see what AJ would look like if male pattern baldness set in.

The next day, the adults went grocery shopping in preparation for my mother's cooking lessons. I'm sure my aunt was relieved, because the previous night, my mother had served one of her signature dishes: hot dogs on stale buns.

I wagged my tail in anticipation when my mother and her sister arrived home, carrying armloads of groceries as they entered through the basement door. Although I was happy about food being brought into the house—I always am—it was the thought of what the two of them would discover in the house that had me in such a happy state. I watched their faces with uncontained glee.

The Millionaire Mind

1. Determine What You Want.

2. Find a Way to Get
   Around Obstacles.

3. Enjoy the Spoils
   of Winning.

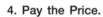

4. Pay the Price.

163

"Eww. It smells like poop in here," my mother said.

"Yeah, like a poop factory!" Aunt Catcollector confirmed.

Unbeknownst to the two of them, my feline sister Moose was clogged and leaking out poo juice. She had wandered from floor to floor dripping like a leaky faucet during their absence.

My mother soon located Moose's trail—not a fun trail that you go hiking on in the woods, but more like a trail through a sewage purifying station. It started on the love seat in the basement. There, a diarrhea spot on the leather cushion extended across the couch, onto the arm support, continuing on the floor, out the room, through the hallway, and up the stairs.

Putting the grocery bags down, the two sisters followed the path up the stairs and into the living room area, and I stayed close on their heels. There, on the formal couch and chairs, were more of Moose's anal tracks. By the looks of things, she couldn't get comfortable on any one piece of furniture so she tried them all.

"I'm going to kill that cat!" my mother cried.

They picked up the scent again on the stairwell leading to the second floor. The sisters followed Moose's trail of shame to the guest bedroom. Inside, Moose lay on the guest bed, next to a puddle of poo.

Turning to her sister, all my mother said was, "I'm glad that's not my bed," and then walked away laughing.

"But I'm a guest!"

"You're not a guest, you're my sister."

So far the visit was going relatively well. I mean nobody had died . . . yet.

The next morning, I awakened to an uncontrollable itch on my stomach. I had been delinquent in moisturizing my skin, so I vowed to do a better job lest I continue to suffer the consequences. But by that evening, Copper started to scratch herself incessantly. At first, I thought it was related to one of her many allergies. But when I noticed my parents sleeping in their beds, scratching, I knew something wasn't right. I had a suspicion as to the cause but I didn't say anything for fear I would get blamed.

The following morning, I heard my aunt telling my mother that she and my uncle had been scratching themselves all night.

"That's funny because we're itchy, too!" my mother exclaimed. Suddenly they both came to the same conclusion.

"Are you using a new detergent?" my aunt asked.

"Yes!" my mother exclaimed.

"I bet we're allergic to it."

"I think you're right."

I shook my head. Neither one of these two would ever be a Sherlock Holmes, or even a Maxwell Smart for that matter.

It wasn't until my mother noticed all three dogs scratching themselves that it finally dawned on her.

"You know what? I don't think it's the detergent at all, I think we have fleas in the house!"

Without warning, she grabbed me and rolled me onto my back. In an instant they spotted black little critters feasting on my soft, yet supple skin.

The paw pointing began. "Well Bo and Copper have never had fleas so I know it wasn't them. AJ must have brought them here," my mother charged.

Her sister countered, "I don't think so. We treat AJ for fleas so I know he doesn't have them. It had to be *your* dogs."

"No, it couldn't be Bo or Copper. How do you explain that we've been living in this house for years and we've never had fleas until you brought your dog here?"

"All I know is that we bathed AJ before we got here, so I know it wasn't him."

Back and forth they went just like stubborn sisters do, ending with no resolution, while I stood by, miserable, biting my belly every minute or so. Moose took it all in from a distance, not offering up the fact she had just been at the local flea market to purchase some catnip.

The sisters devised a plan: fumigate and eradicate. They gave us flea baths and doused us with chemicals akin to Agent Orange. But while the house was undergoing fumigation, we all got to go for an unexpected ride. Yippee!

We piled into the Caravan: four humans, three dogs, and one cat. Accommodations were tight, but cozy. We drove away, a cacophony of voices, barks, and meows roaring out the lone open window.

Copper, having difficulty getting comfortable, jumped from one side of the van to the other before finally settling on a spot between my mother and the door. As Copper settled into position, my mother reached under her so she wouldn't sit on the bulky, retractable leash. My mother wasn't quick enough; Copper sat on the leash and my mother's hand.

Pulling her arm out from underneath Copper, my mother asked, "Why is the leash wet?"

A smell filled the van.

It was then that my mother noticed a big brown spot on the back of her hand. Copper had just expressed her anal glands.

For the uninitiated, the odor was a cross between tuna that's been left out in the sun for a week and rotten eggs sprinkled with Parmesan cheese. To the canine nose, this odiferous bouquet is quite delectable. For humans? Not so much.

My mother screamed, "I have anal juice on my hands! Pull over! I'm gonna be sick! Pull over! Pull over!"

The van stopped at the side of the road to let everyone out. After a fifteen-minute break to air out the van and to let my mother wipe her hands with a pile of Wet-Naps, AJ turned to me and gave me a look that said, "I don't think I'll be coming back next year."

Considering everything that happened, I couldn't blame him. Come to think of it, I wouldn't blame my uncle, either.

When the Catcollectors finally left I was sorry to see them go. They had infused our lives with excitement. But I sensed the feeling wasn't mutual.

Unfortunately my mother didn't learn any new recipes or proper dinner party etiquette from her sister. There was no helping her. She would need to be comfortable in what she was; a one-trick pony with four-star aspirations.

CHAPTER 22

Ain't Gonna Be No Rematch

I'm not one to play games. Physical games, that is; I love playing mental ones. I never saw the point in chasing a ball or a stick only to bring it back to the person who threw it. If it's such a precious thing, why was it thrown?

If I want exercise I'll break out of the yard, or in a pinch, have my parents walk me. I don't need to be humiliated by being told to chase something.

The only game I ever really enjoyed was tug-of-war. When I was a pup, I couldn't get enough of that game. I was great at it, too.

But I'm getting older, and I've given up on tug-of-war, for the most part. I'm a bit weary of the old man pulling too hard on the tuggie rope. The last thing I need is my dentures falling out. Besides, there are other games to play; they just don't include my father.

In the spring of '03, I was a pathetic 0 for 432. This statistic refers to the number of squirrels I'd caught versus the number I'd chased. Not a good track record, especially for a canine who prides himself on results.

On a glorious Saturday morning, I was presented with an opportunity to stop the streak as Copper and I patrolled the backyard.

We'd been walking the beat for a few minutes, Copper starting on one side of the yard and I on the other. Initial surveillance of the area indicated not much had changed from the previous evening, when a subtle movement in the middle of the yard set off alarm bells in my head. There, in the free and clear, stood Rocky, the leader of the neighborhood squirrels.

With Copper on one side of the yard and I on the other, our chance of success doubled. I gave immediate chase, and Copper joined in, thus mounting a clever bidirectional attack that momentarily confused Rocky. He hesitated a mere moment before sprinting toward the closest tree, but alas, it was a moment too long.

I got to Rocky first. Dizzy with excitement, I grabbed him and shook him side to side like a Polaroid picture. Copper skidded to a stop and whimpered, bummed at having been a few seconds too late to the party. Not wanting her to miss out on the excitement of the moment, I tossed Rocky her way so she could have some fun.

Copper was hesitant; this was a new game for her. At first, she took him gently in her mouth and shook him slowly. After a few moments, she had gained her confidence and began thrashing him around. She then sent him airborne back my way. And so it went, back and forth. What a fun game!

As Copper took another turn, I looked toward the house and saw our parents through the window. As if on cue, they looked up and spotted us with Rocky. Shrieks of horror filled the air as the back door flew open, and they sprinted toward us, determined to stop our game of Hot Potato Squirrel.

My father pried Rocky from Copper's mouth while my mother grabbed me by the collar and escorted me away from the scene of the crime, yelling in the melodramatic way I've come to love and expect from her.

You'd think we killed her precious azalea bush the way she was carrying on.

Once inside, I peeked out the closest window. Rocky had not fared well from our encounter. He appeared to have lost the use of his back legs, evidenced most notably when he tried to climb the tree only to come tumbling back down. Despite my triumph over catching him, I felt a little remorse. My parents were devastated.

My mother made a series of phone calls to vets, animal societies, and shamans alike to determine the best course of action. Unfortunately it appeared that Rock's future wasn't looking so bright. After quite an effort, she finally found an animal hospital willing to euthanize Rocky. Bullwinkle would be crushed to lose his TV buddy, but the suffering needed to end.

While my mother scribbled down directions to the animal hospital, my father captured Rocky and loaded him into the truck. Then they drove out of sight, leaving me to wonder about the fate of my furry friend.

As my father told me later, getting Rocky relieved of his pain wasn't as easy as it could have been.

After a short drive to the executioner's palace, they walked in with box in hand. As one would expect on a Saturday, the clinic was jam packed with pets and owners. Even so, it appeared my father's box contained the only squirrel in the place.

My mother approached the woman behind the counter and indicated she was the one who called about Rocky.

The receptionist didn't seem to understand. "I'm sorry. You're here about what?"

"I called you about a squirrel that was maimed by my dogs."

"You called us? You didn't speak to me about it. I would have remembered that."

"Well, I spoke with someone here. They told me to bring the squirrel in. It's paralyzed."

"Let me find out who you spoke to."

The receptionist went to find out who took the call in the same manner a twelve-year-old checks to make sure his sister is coming down for dinner.

"Hey, did anybody talk to a lady about a paralyzed squirrel?" she screamed to the technicians in the back. "She's got it here in a box and she says it needs help."

By this time everyone in the room was watching the drama unfold; their faces were contorted in a "you gotta be kidding me" look. Turns out that in Georgia, people shoot squirrels; they don't try to minimize their pain.

After some giggles and an awkward silence, one of the technicians in the back responded, "No. Nobody back here talked to anyone about a squirrel."

Turning to my mother the lady behind the counter asked, "I'm sorry I can't help you. Are you sure you got the right place, ma'am?"

"This is Cobb Emergency Vet Clinic, isn't it?"

"No, ma'am. That's up the street a few miles."

Humiliated, my father got out of there as fast as he could with my mother hot on his tail. No word on what Rocky felt.

Ten minutes later, they arrived at the correct facility.

The folks at the clinic were very kind and took the box from my father's hands. My parents inquired whether they needed to pay for anything and were told they didn't. However, if they were so inclined, a donation to the wildlife society would be very much appreciated.

So what does one owe society for the maiming of a squirrel, inflicting an afternoon's worth of emotional pain on it, and ultimately sending it to the big oak tree in the sky?

By my mother's calculations, that's worth $10.

Rocky died that day, and so did the streak. I was now 1 for 433.

CHAPTER 23

Creature Feature

Columbus has his, Martin Luther King Jr. has one, too, and Washington and Lincoln have one dedicated to them as well. What is it? A day devoted to their lives and a celebration of their contributions to the world.

Although the aforementioned have their twenty-four hours in the sun every year, they have nothing on my mother. You see, she has more days dedicated to her than even a fuzzy little creature I like to call me.

There's her birthday and then her birth month, Valentine's Day and Valentine's Week, and the never to be forgotten anniversary weekend. There's also the day my parents first met, the day of their first date, and the day they got engaged. There are other days, too, and the expectation is that, at a minimum, a card is forthcoming from my father to acknowledge each of the "special" days. A quick look at my desk calendar and it appears that April 23 is the only day not dedicated to her.

For what it's worth, I let my father sleep in on that day.

I remember one of the first Valentine's Days I was a part of when my father tried to get by with giving my mother a card only. There was nothing wrong with the gesture other than the fact it was a card made on his computer and output on a cheap ink-jet printer. It was quite evident to everyone but him that this was a last-ditch effort to cover up the fact he forgot about this most important day, or that he was too lazy to go to the store to get a card. Either way, it was a bad reflection on him. Even I was forced to slink out of the room when he gave it to her.

There's also the story my mother tells of their first Christmas present exchange after falling in love. She searched high and low looking for that special gift to give him. He did the same. When he opened his gift to find a most beautiful watch, he was ecstatic. When she opened her present, she was less so. What did my father get the first woman he ever loved?

A sweatshirt.

A sweatshirt with Opus the cartoon character on it.

Clearly, my father was card- and gift-giving challenged. He bought cards, in bulk, in single shopping sprees at the local Hallmark store ("In case of emergency, Bo. You never want to be caught short-handed.") that he would use for years until they ran out. In a pinch he was known to change the word *Valentine* to *Anniversary*, or *From All of Us* to *From All of Me*, or even changing the word *Congratulations* to *Happy Birthday*. And he always signed them, "Your friend—me."

There were also the rare instances he'd buy jewelry for my mother, only to have it be returned for something a bit more tasteful, and expensive. There was the $400 vacuum cleaner he bought her; it was Valentine's Day, after all. It was promptly returned. Not discouraged, he bought a Roomba for her birthday that year. Yes, that's a robotic vacuum cleaner. For whatever reason, he just didn't get it.

Until the times he did. There were the unannounced weekend getaways, the unexpected Easter candy shrines, and the surprise flower deliveries he seemed to pull out of thin air.

The thing was, my mother never knew which version of my father was in charge of the next gift-getting occasion.

So it was and, I suspect, so it will forever be.

Erratic gift giving is something my father had in common with my sister Moose.

Even though I've spent a lot of time with Moose over the years, I don't think I ever fully understood cats. One of their idiosyncrasies is that they bring "things" to their owners to show their love. Not cool things like Frisbees or tennis balls, but things that crawl around in the backyard. To me, if it's worth chasing and catching, it's worth keeping yourself. If you really want to show your love, just lie there and wag your tail once, maybe twice a day. That would show true love, but cats are different and do things in their own way.

The bizarre behavior of felines isn't easily understood, even by humans, and this was the source of the strained relationship between Moose and my mother. Don't get me wrong, my mother loved Moose, just not every minute of every day. Jumping up on the kitchen counter and licking the just-made chicken, regardless of how dry and over-cooked it is, is going to lead to tension.

To complicate matters, my mother was also responsible for emptying Moose's bedpan, even if Copper or I had already snatched the good stuff first. I don't care how much you love someone, if you have to clean up their pee and poop every day, there's going to be some level of resentment and conflict.

To her credit, Moose knew this. She did her best to stay in my mother's good graces, it's just that she didn't tailor her message to the recipient. Hadn't she learned anything in cat school?

But try she did. How do I know? By the array of presents my sister Moose delivered to my mother via Feline

Express. Invariably, these gifts were of the dead and head-less animal variety, and delivered when my father was out of town, leaving my mother to sign for the packages all by herself.

One of the bad habits my mother got into upon moving to Georgia was leaving the back door open. She often did this during the spring and fall seasons to allow the pleas-ant breeze to flow through the house, and to air out the musty smell of my cabbage farts. It didn't take long for my mother to pay for her lapse in judgment by allowing Moose such easy access to the outdoors.

Shortly after we moved in, Moose gave my mother a half-eaten mouse (whom I affectionately dubbed Meatloaf) as a housewarming gift. I suspect he was left under my parents' bed because my sister didn't have time to wrap him up. Although Moose's shameless sucking-up put me off, I have to admit that watching my mother's reaction to the gift was worth my aggravation.

After the shrieking subsided, my mother stuck a bucket on one side of the bed, and took a broom to the other side of the bed, where she proceeded to get down on her hands and knees, using the broom to maneuver the chewed up mouse into the bucket. It was like a carnival game. After several attempts, my mother managed to get Meatloaf lined up in front of the bucket, requiring just one last "poke." Unfortunately she missed, and her last thrust pushed the rodent into the rim of the bucket, causing it to roll away. This happened several times before she escorted Meatloaf to his resting place in the backyard. My mother cursed Moose the entire time, which I thought was ungrateful of her. Moose, however, took great joy in having given a pres-ent that occupied so much of her mother's time.

Chipmunks weren't safe from Moose's obsessive shop-ping, either. After stalking her prey she would bring them home, dropping them at my mother's feet. If the back door was closed, Moose left them to bake in the hot Georgia sun, topless. Topless in this instance just means headless. My mother thought it was bad enough scraping up a half-eaten critter and throwing it away, but her bigger concern was the location of the head. I was concerned, too. The head is the really good part, the chewy center in the middle, if you will. You'd hate to see that go to waste.

Sometimes the goodwill gesture was lucky enough to be delivered to our home alive. One such fortunate chipmunk (whom I dubbed Simon) lived with us for two days. Somehow Moose captured him on patrol in the jungles of our backyard and brought him back alive. In a daring escape plan, Simon broke free from his captor and hid inside the house. It wasn't long before my mother discovered him. Moose was escorted to the cat holding area, the laundry room, so she couldn't kill him. For the next few hours, Simon the chipmunk played a rousing game of hide-and-seek with my mother and Copper. My father? Out of town. Me? Eh, my bones were a little achy and quite frankly I just wasn't up to the drama. Getting older will do that to you.

A few hours into this unscheduled visit, my mother was in the living room, pretending to watch TV. But I could tell by the nervous way she flicked through the channels that she was panicked about Simon. As if on cue, Simon scrambled from behind the overstuffed chair to the corner table and then wandered behind the curtain. My mother was scared to get up for fear the chipmunk would rush at her and kill her. She was a prisoner on her own couch. She slept there that night.

It wasn't until the following afternoon when a hero finally emerged. That hero was Copper. Being the gentle giant she is, Copper hunted Simon down in the corner of the room and gently took him in her mouth. Coaxing Copper outside, my

Great Names in History

Gassious Clay   Even the greatest boxer of all time appreciates the power of a well placed stink bomb.

Winnie the Poo   The last name says it all.

Pee Wee Herman   Was Pee Alot taken?

Bo Jackson   Two things I have in common with him; his name and his talent.

Dog the Bounty Hunter   What you gonna do when they come for you?

Seymour Butts   If you ain't the lead dog, the view never changes.

James Caanine   You don't mess with Sonny Corleone's family any more than you want to mess with mine.

Dogbert   The classic working-class hero.

Deputy Dawg   What I would have been in the Old West.

Superman's not as great a name as SuperBo.

mother had her spit Simon out at the back edge of the yard. Once dropped, the chipmunk scurried off and would, no doubt, go on to tell great tales of his adventures with the big silly creatures that lived in the funny looking tree house. It was game over, just minutes before my father came home.

"Hey, how's it going? Anything exciting happen?" my father said as he put his suitcase down on the bed.

"Moose brought in a killer chipmunk that's been terrorizing me the last two days!" my mother exclaimed. "I told you we needed a screen door for the back. You need to put it on tomorrow."

"Why didn't you just leave the door closed?"

"Because it's nice out."

The next day my father installed a screen door to stop the comings and goings of wildlife from the house. This do-it-yourself project put quite a damper on my ability to sneak outside and lick the drippings from the grill.

The good news was the door my parents had installed was really cheap, like $24.99 cheap. It took me only three tries to rip out the lower part of the screen. My father hastily fixed it, but in a matter of minutes I walked through it again, breaking it. That was my grill juice out there and I wasn't going to let a silly old screen stop me. My father realized this, too, and stopped fixing the door.

Having resolved our outdoor access issues, we were able to focus on important stuff, like things we love in the wilderness. I'm fond of bunnies; Moose is, too.

In fact she loves to play with them. One Saturday afternoon when I was locked in the house, I watched from the basement windows as Moose pursued a little rabbit (whom I dubbed Rudy) in the backyard. She hovered over him, waiting for him to move. When he did, she pounced, making sure to keep him between her paws. She'd lie down, wait for him to move again, and play out the same scenario over and over again. In the nick of time my parents noticed the game Moose was playing, too, and grabbed her before she could do any major damage.

They brought Moose inside and closed the door to the bunny ranch outside.

Now I'm not saying Rudy was stupid, but I'd be remiss if I didn't tell you that he was probably a few carrots short of a bunch. Had it been me I would have been off into the woods and on my way home. Not Rudy; he just sat there holding his "Get Out of Kitty's Teeth Free" card, oblivious to the dangers still around him.

My parents, too, remained oblivious to the dangers still around as they stood in the basement and gloated over their rescue.

"How big of a place in heaven you think we get for saving him?" my father said with his chest puffed to twice its normal size.

"It's gotta be pretty big. That was one cute bunny," my mother chimed in.

"And he was a baby bunny. That's extra points if you ask me. Who knows what he'll grow up to be? We may have changed the course of history!"

"I think we get a penthouse suite from the Guy in the Sky for this one."

"We're such suckers for animals."

"I know. We're such good people."

Finished with the self-congratulatory conversation, my mother turned to go upstairs. When she did, she nearly tripped over Moose and the furry present she held between her paws—Rudy! A dead Rudy!

It was a very *Fatal Attraction* kind of moment.

A shriek of horror drifted out of our windows and across the neighborhood. How did this happen? How could Moose have managed to get out of the house, find Rudy, kill him, bring him back, and drop him at my mother's feet? This was an unsolved mystery worthy of Robert Stack.

Worthy, that is, until my father glanced at the open window in the room next door. Moose had jumped out the window and gone shopping for my mother. Unfortunately for Rudy, the return policy was everlasting peace.

And so it was that many of God's creatures were all delivered, at one time or another, as a show of respect to my mother. From a wildlife point of view, my mother was the grim reaper; the only difference was that instead of a sickle, she had a shovel to scrape 'em and bag 'em before casting them off to eternity.

And that penthouse suite in the sky . . . still available.

CHAPTER 24

Just Say No

Nancy Reagan had it right. Just bark "no" to drugs. Unfortunately for my family, it was something we were incapable of.

As I've gotten older, grayer, and achier, it seems I've downed every kind of pill known to dog; be it Rimadyl, Cosequin, glucosamine chondroitin, daily aspirins, or doggie vitamins. That doesn't include the painkillers, antibiotics, and antidepressants that certain "incidents" forced upon me. The good part about my pill regimen is that each one gets covered in something delectable; otherwise it gets spit out on the floor. The routine has evolved to where my mother pulls out her JIF Pill Air Gun and aims it at my mouth.

Fire away, honey, you ain't gonna hurt me.

Copper is on a first name basis with the local pharmacy, too. She needs eye cream for her inverted eyelashes, ear cream for her ear infections, and ice cream for her belly. She also partakes in a daily vitamin regimen, and during allergy season, prescription meds. Oh, and her anal glands need squeezing every other week. There's no pill for that, just strong fingers.

Metamucil Moose gets a hefty dose of unbinding powder mixed into her food every day. When a good old-fashioned neighborhood beatdown takes place, a few containers worth of antibiotics are added to the inventory.

As one can imagine, my mother has a stockpile of goodies, too: vitamin D, vitamin C, nerve blocker pills, multivitamins, allergy medicine, nasal sprays, on and on and on.

Even my father is in on the act, taking a daily aspirin and "gummy" vitamins.

Needless to say, our kitchen counter looks like a pharmacy buffet. And when you've got that many users in one house, things are bound to get out of control.

It was springtime in Paris, and in Georgia, too; allergy season was upon us. My mother's nose dripped like a faucet without a washer. A pollen count in excess of 3,000 parts per million will do that to people. So every day, my mother took her Allegra and gave me my Rimadyl at the same time. She's very organized when it comes to pill distribution.

Maybe she should have been a pharmacist.

You would think with all the practice my mother had downing pills, she would have been good at it. Not so. She had a gag reflex that forced her to break pills in half lest she require the Heimlich maneuver to remove the "enormous" pills from her esophagus. Countless times I told her to try the Jif Gun, but she wouldn't listen.

Anyway, one particular Tuesday morning she laid out our respective pills, took half of her pill, then wandered into the other room to catch a few minutes of *Oprah*, leaving me jonesing for my peanut butter pill treat.

After Oprah was finished spreading her daily goodness, my mother returned to the kitchen and was shocked to discover that my pill was gone and both parts of hers were still there. She realized then that she had taken my pill!

What a selfish owner. What about me and my pain?

Ever the drama queen, my mother launched into a dramatic

monologue, leaving me pill-less and in pain. "Holy cow! I took the dog pill! I need to call the vet to see what's going to happen to me." Then she shook her head.

"I can't call the vet. How can I explain I took the dog pill by mistake? I could call the emergency room but I think I'd rather just die than let them know what I did," she reasoned out loud.

As she continued she became more frantic. "I think I'm having hot flashes! Just walk it off. Just walk it off. I'll be okay. Walk it off."

After some tense moments my mother eventually calmed down, and monitored herself through the rest of the day and well into the night.

Waking the next day, she was pretty sure she was going to make it through unscathed, except for the emotional toll it took on her psyche.

And the constant need to have my father rub her belly.

A week after this episode, I went upstairs to be with my mother in the bedroom, this time to watch a Lifetime movie. Maybe you've seen it, it's where a wife is abused by her husband and gets revenge in the end.

So we were curled up in bed when I heard my father come home. I knew he'd be looking to snack on something, so I headed downstairs. Sure enough, he gave me my peanut butter–laden pill, along with a piece of cheese. Both were tasty, and well worth the trip down the stairs. After my father finished his peanut butter and banana sandwich we went back upstairs to the bedroom, ready to lie down and retire for the evening.

Once we were settled in bed, my mother asked my father, "Can you give Bo his pill?"

"I just gave it to him."

With a strange look on her face my mother responded, "No, you didn't. His pill is right there on the dresser."

"I gave him the one you laid out on the counter down-stairs."

"That wasn't for him, that pill was for me. It was my nerve blocker!"

What!? It was one of her pills? This wasn't good. Her medicine was so strong it had been known to kill cattle. Now it was coursing through my veins? Holy crap, they drugged me.

Was this their way of getting me hooked on drugs, to have a lifelong junkie on their hands willing to do anything for a fix?

I could see it now, "Bo, you know you wanna get high. I'll help you if you play dead, or roll over or . . ."

Before I knew it I'd be balancing a biscuit on my nose waiting for the command to catch it and eat it. They were trying to trick me into being a good dog! They slipped me a Mickey for their own benefit. These people had no soul!

A heavy daze enveloped my head and I could barely think. My face felt droopy; my eyelids weighed a thousand pounds. My massive cranium became heavier and heavier. I didn't know where I was, who I was, or what I was. I fell into a disturbing sleep.

Barker's Beauties were off in the distance as Bob approached me in his neutering outfit. I ran, but everything was happening in slow motion, and Bob was about to set the right price on my privates . . .

The crowd was quiet with anticipation. I was panting with excitement.

"For a million dollars, is that your final answer?" Regis asked.

"Ruuf"

"Final answer?"

"Ruuf"

"I'm sorry, but the answer was floor."

"This is final jeopardy," boomed Alex Trebec.
"The answer is: 'Ma Kettle's better half.'"

Cue the music: Do do do do do do do, do do do do dut do do do do do du

"Bo, if you get this correct you will be our new Jeopardy *champion and end Ken Jennings's reign. Your response?"*

I slowly reveal my answer in anticipation of my win:

"I'm sorry but you did not phrase it in a question. The correct question is: What is paw?

"Ken Jennings remains our champion."

The board read: C A ____
The clue: A household animal.

"Give the wheel a spin, Bo," said Pat Sajak. The wheel slowed, passing the $1,000 slot, then Peanut Butter for Life, nearly stopping on the $5,000 opening before clicking over to "Bankrupt."

"No whammy, no whammy, Stop!"

And this finally woke me from my dreams.
"He's up!" my mother said.

"Wow, he slept a straight forty-eight hours without getting up. Even the Game Show channel's marathon couldn't get him up," my father responded. "I guess the vet was right. He was just going to be a bit sleepy."

A bit sleepy? It felt as if I'd fallen asleep before Rip Van Winkle, gotten up after him, and still needed a nap.

At least I was awake and away from those dastardly dreams.

I knew I was the victim of an honest mistake, but now I always look twice when a peanut butter pill comes my way.

Our kitchen pharmacy never lost its license, but it did make me think, maybe my mother shouldn't be the pharmacist after all.

CHAPTER 25

The Butcher of Burnham Way

I lay alone in the corner of the living room, exhausted from the flurry of activity I had just been through. My gray face and creaky body hadn't been that energetic in years. I was worn out and covered in blood.

It wasn't long before I dozed off. Flashes of odd things popped in and out of my dream. There was blood and garbage, cat food and human food, and kitty litter.

Like most dreams, it didn't make sense.

When I awoke, I was in an interrogation room. A bright light pierced my eyes, though I could still make out a shadowy figure pacing in the background. The temperature in the room was hot, Africa hot. My mouth was bone dry, but my requests for a bowl of water were repeatedly ignored, and no matter how much I begged, there were no treats forthcoming.

"Bo, come on now. Just get it off your chest and you'll feel a lot better," said the shadow. "You have no alibi; witnesses have stated they saw you around the scene of the crime, plus you had every motive to commit this offense."

"Shouldn't I have a lawyer here?" I asked.

"I'm sure he's on his way. In the meantime just tell us what you were doing around six this evening?"

I knew what I had done was wrong. I had done it many times before but hadn't suffered any serious penalties, and had never fully anticipated the consequences of my actions. On this occasion, I wasn't so lucky. There was blood all over the house. It was on the floor, the windowpanes, the wall, and the front door. The only thing missing was the victim's body.

"I was sleeping, waiting for my parents to come home. I don't know how the blood got everywhere," I said, swallowing hard.

"Liar! You killed something, Bo. The evidence is all around. Look at the blood on the walls, on the floor, on the windows! How did you do it? Did you tear up the victim with your mouth or just chop it up with the doggie hair clippers? Come clean and you'll feel a whole lot better."

"I . . . I don't know what you're talking about. I was napping all afternoon."

"Are you trying to tell me that you slept through this bloody rampage? C'mon, be serious. The place was ransacked. Look at all the garbage strewn about. You want us to believe you were napping peacefully while this took place?"

"I'm a deep sleeper."

Yes, I had knocked over the garbage pail. Yes, it was me that picked through it. Yes, I tossed it about the house, but I didn't kill anything. It's just that I was heeding advice that had been imparted to me years earlier by a wily old dog: never, ever admit to being guilty.

The interrogator had had enough. "Okay, if that's the way you want to play it, fine."

He stopped the verbal tongue-lashing and became physical. A strong hand pushed me down on the floor, followed by the weight of a heavy body covering me. I couldn't move.

I was scared. What was his plan? A wet willy? A fishhook?

No, it was much worse. He tickled my toe fur.

Just a little tickle at first, barely noticeable. But after re-peated soft brushes from a finger and the intensity grew. I curled my paws to no avail. In a matter of seconds I was a broken dog.

"Okay. I admit it. It was me who knocked over the garbage pail. There was the sweet smell of old chili combined with some rotting mushrooms that were driving me crazy. You can't expect to put a dog in a position to smell that and not do anything about it. I knocked it over in the laundry room and threw the garbage around looking for more good stuff to eat."

"You're not telling me the whole truth are you, Bo?" I was given a little fur tickle to help me come clean.

"Yes, I am."

"Well, how do you explain the blood then? It's every-where, especially in the area that you have now confessed to being at."

"Chili and mushrooms, that's all I wanted."

"Sure, now you say that chili and mushrooms are all you wanted. Just a few minutes ago you were telling me you were one hundred percent innocent. Tell me the truth, you didn't stop with the chili and mushrooms did you? Did you?"

"I might have had some leftover salsa and some rotting asparagus spears, too."

"You would have me believe that you were only after rotting human garbage? Is that correct?"

"Yes, it's the truth."

"You make me sick!" the shadow yelled before leaving the room.

I chewed on my paw, trying to calm my nerves. I wasn't telling the whole truth but it was pretty close; I was just looking for human garbage. But once I got through with the first course I wanted more. I couldn't stop myself.

Man, was I thirsty. I'd do anything for some toilet water right now.

The door opened slowly and I could make out the figure of a woman, petite in stature but imposing in posture.

"Why, Bo? Why? You get everything you want and then some, but once you're left to your own devices you do something evil. Your parents are always left to clean up your wrongs."

Hey, I wasn't evil, just persistent in the things I want. This time wasn't any different except the blood.

I said nothing.

"So you don't want to talk, huh?"

She turned and yelled to someone outside the room. "Get it ready!"

I heard a chilling sound from outside the room. It wasn't the sound of a voice or a bark but that of a bath being drawn. These people were cold blooded.

"All right, I'll talk. After I ate the human food I went into the cat litter and ate the cat's poop. I need the protein, for crying out loud. My daily rations just aren't cutting it."

"I am well aware of you hitting the kitty litter buffet, Bo. I can smell your breath from a mile away. Tell me, what else haven't you been totally upfront about or would you rather take a bath?"

It was to no avail. I might as well be totally honest.

"After I ate the rotting garbage and gave myself a kitty snicker treat I couldn't stop. It's not that I was hungry; I just enjoy food. You don't understand, the more I get, the more I need. Let me tell ya, I needed more so I went in the pantry. At the bottom of the pantry are small, unopened cans of cat food. I couldn't get to the can opener because it sits so high on the counter so I opened them with my teeth."

"Weren't you afraid of cutting yourself?"

"You just don't get it, do you? Once you're under the influence of a food-induced rampage, nothing will stop you. I once heard of a little Yorkie lifting a tractor off a sack of Milkbones trapped underneath just so she could eat those treats. Food is a major drug that does strange things to you. In my mind I knew I wasn't going to cut myself on the cans."

"So you opened the cat cans with your mouth?"

I nodded, hanging my head in guilt.

"So, that leaves us with one last thing. Where's the body?"

"What body?"

"The body that contained all the blood that's spread around the house. Since you indicated you did not cut yourself on the sharp edges of the cat food cans, it had to have come from somewhere else."

"There is nobody. The blood is mine. Although my mind knew I wasn't going to cut myself by chewing the cans open, my body had other ideas. I cut my mouth on the cans. I lost a lot of blood but fortunately by the time I got light-headed I had finished eating. All the blood around the house is mine. You can take a swab of my mouth for DNA confirmation if you want."

"So you didn't kill anything?"

"No, but if it makes you feel better, you can call me the Butcher of Burnham Way." The woman turned the light off and left the room, returning a short time later with a bowl of water. The interrogation was over.

My parents didn't understand why I did what I did, but they accepted it anyway. In return, I accepted them even though they continued to throw food away. It's the least we could do for each other.

Later that night, I overheard my father say, "I hope no-body ever gets accused of murder in this house because if they shine a black light on the walls they're going to think this place was a slaughterhouse."

Did someone say slaughterhouse? I'm hungry again.

CHAPTER 26

Treasure Island

Treasure.

It's buried in my front yard, right under the front porch. To the naked eye, or unobservant human, it doesn't exist at all. For a well-trained hound like me, it is as apparent as a T-bone on the kitchen floor. My well-honed olfactory senses pick up on the treasure as quickly as a metal detector picks up coins on a beach. Like Jack Russell Sparrow, my goal is to get at it.

So what is this treasure I speak of?

It is loot from the kitty krowd. I feel no pangs of guilt or remorse in my everlasting quest to steal it from them.

The cats come, day by day, one by one, to bury their goods, thinking it safe from the world at large. But what they don't know is that I watch, and I smell, and I know where their treasure lies.

All I need is the opportunity.

Recently, when my father was out of town and my mother had an engagement that would keep her out late, they asked our neighbor Lou to look after me. My mother's instructions were simple enough: "Just let Bo out the front door to pee on the lawn, and fill up his water bowl and food bowl. All his stuff is in the kitchen."

Did you catch that? I was now allowed to pee on the

front lawn. The reason was that I was starting to feel the aches and pains in my bones as Father Time took his toll. My parents had noticed and figured instead of having me climb up and down the steep stairs at the back of the house, I only had to take on two of them in the front. They also allowed me to do this off leash, since they were now faster than me. I had to face facts; I wasn't a spring chicken anymore, so I appreciated the gesture.

Even though I had slowed physically, I was still sharp mentally, especially when pitted against a dogless—and therefore clueless—neighbor.

"Don't worry. I got it taken care of," was his response to my mother's request. As you may remember, Lou was a rotund man with more belly than brain—a fact I was determined to take full advantage of.

"Whatever you do, don't let him go under the porch or you'll never get him out of there," were the last words of warning my mother gave him. Maybe they should have been the first.

Moose, Copper, and I spent a quiet afternoon lounging around the house, enjoying the peace and quiet. It wasn't until the winter tilt of the earth ensured that darkness had fallen on our little corner of the world that I heard footsteps shuffling onto the front porch and the jingling of keys in the lock. The front door swung open, revealing my neighbor, and for today, my stooge.

As I had been waiting for some time to do my business, his arrival was most welcome. With his encouragement I walked out the front door to pee, just waiting for my chance to take advantage of his trusting nature. There was treasure in them there hills, I mean under the porch, and I had the map to find it.

When my sister Cooper diverted his attention, I made a beeline for the opening under the porch. Well, in my younger

States I've Peed In

(by Volume of Pee)

Quiz! Can you identify the state by its shape and the aggregate pee amount I left in that state?

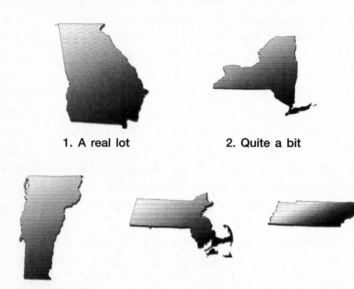

1. A real lot

2. Quite a bit

3. Enough to fer-
tilize a lawn

4. A nice downpour

5. Summer drizzle

days, it would have been a beeline, but nowadays, it's more like a slow saunter, but you get the point. As I wriggled my way under the porch, the neighbor called out.

"Bo. Come on, Bo, let's go inside."

I ignored him, delicately scratching the surface of the dirt with my paws.

"Bo? Bo, where are you?"

I ignored him, sensing I was close to becoming a very rich hound. My heartbeat quickened. My digging paws accelerated.

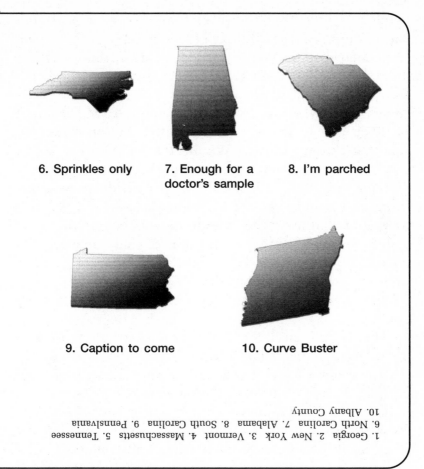

6. Sprinkles only

7. Enough for a doctor's sample

8. I'm parched

9. Caption to come

10. Curve Buster

1. Georgia 2. New York 3. Vermont 4. Massachusetts 5. Tennessee 6. North Carolina 7. Alabama 8. South Carolina 9. Pennsylvania 10. Albany County

Having gone inside the house, the dog-sitter quickly returned with my dinner bowl. Instead of calling me, he began banging my bowl with a spoon. Apparently this was his way to entice me to come out. Amateur.

"Where's that damn dog? Bo, where are you? Baoooh!"

His yelling almost disturbed my Indiana Jones moment. Almost.

He left again, only to come back with a flashlight. After scouring the yard, he finally flashed the light under the porch and onto the ground in front of me, thus illuminating the most beautiful cache of treasure I'd ever seen. I had uncovered the mother load of . . . kitty manna. Stacked three deep and covering at least twenty square feet, the area was covered with cat poo. This was indeed the legendary place where all cat poo went to die. To me, it wasn't so much a cemetery as it was a buffet. My only concern was that I'd end up like Winnie the Pooh in the honey tree—too fat to squeeze out from under the porch.

I knew my time was short, so I scarfed down as many treats as I could. My dog-sitter, having realized where I was hiding but not what I was hiding on, got on his hands and knees to retrieve me. He was saying some unkind words, surely trying to use reverse psychology, to coax me from my spot but to no avail.

When he finally reached me, the smell gave him quite a jolt.

"This is cat crap! I'm crawling around in cat crap!" And then after looking at me, he said, "And you're eating it!"

Darn straight I was. I was looking for a little balance in my diet. I hadn't had my vitamin shake that day.

He grabbed my collar and dragged me out of my new favorite place, then locked me in the house and left me alone until my mother arrived a few hours later.

I slept well that night, in a kitty poo–induced coma. I didn't even brush my teeth before bed.

The next morning, the neighbor stopped by the house to have a discussion with my mother.

"Bo was a handful last night. Why didn't you tell me not to let him go underneath the porch?" he asked her.

"I did. That was the last thing I told you to be careful of."

"You didn't tell me that. Did you? Are you sure you told me that?"

He paused, then continued. "If you did, you're right;

you shouldn't let him under there. He's almost impossible to get out, plus it's all covered in cat poop."

As she listened to her neighbor, my mother glanced down at his legs, prompting the question, "Why do you have bandages on your knees?"

It was simple, you never get between a dog and his treasure.

CHAPTER 27

Unintended Consequences

Once a year, we receive a visit from my mother's parents, an event I always look forward to.

They were the perfect guests for a dog like me; my grandfather was an early bird who loved to cook and my grandmother was a night owl and a night eater. They were both easily separated from their food with just one pleading look.

I gained ten pounds every time they came to town.

But even perfect guests can have quirks that may get under your coat. The biggest peeve I had was my grandmother's insistence that everything be put into Ziploc bags. I'm not sure why, but she does. A perfect example is cereal. It comes from the factory in a box, containing a bag to keep it fresh. Most people see fit to leave it in there, delving it out one bowl at a time until it's finished. Not her. She pours out the entire contents of the bag and places it inside Ziploc bags. I ask you, once transferred to airtight look-a-like bags, how is a dog to tell the difference between dog chow and Goldfish crackers, cat chow and Pringles, or Boo Berry cereal and All Bran?

He can't, unless it's labeled properly. And ours never is.

I'm sure this bizarre bag behavior has a cure, but if it

doesn't, the mishap that occurred several months later should energize those whose loved ones are afflicted with the same disease into fighting for one.

It began when Marcy Catcollector came for a visit, alone. What I've discovered is that when she is in town, she and my mother will run about town doing all kinds of errands, leaving me alone for good chunks at a time. This gives me ample time to think and to scheme.

On one such occasion, I was lying on the living room floor, thinking about those clear bags of cereal. They were calling, "Bo . . . eat me! I'm tasty . . . eat me!"

They were within reach, enticingly close really, if only the pantry door were left open. A quick check of this door confirmed that it was open a crack. With a swift turn of my snout, I flung the door wide open.

At first it didn't look good for me. The pantry floor was nearly impenetrable, littered with kitchen gadgets and appliances that had outlived their usefulness, or were never useful to begin with.

To the untrained eye, there was no way to get at the bags of cereal, but as you may have imagined, my eyeballs were highly trained. Sure I would need to plan carefully to get at the coveted bags containing the twelve sugar-coated essential vitamins and minerals, but my plan was genius in its simplicity. The key was to climb from one appliance up to the next until the destination was reached.

Here was the plan, in its entirety, as transcribed from my original notes:

1. At the front of the pantry, step on the George Foreman grill that's been placed inside the wok. Be careful, the wok wobbles.

2. Step onto the Ronco Five Tray Food Dehydrator. Don't be distracted by the smell of old jerky coming from

the machine. Keep going but be sure to balance yourself on the ice tea maker by its side.

3, Now carefully step up onto the Juiceman. It is stacked
precariously against the wall. If need be, lean against
the wall to steady yourself.

4. Once stable, take the final step onto the Ronco Ro-
tisserie Model 4000 chicken maker that sits atop the
two Tupperware containers.

5. You should now be able to look up and nudge the
Ziploc bag off the shelf. If not, use the Pocket Fisher-
man in your fur suit to pull the bags toward you.

6. Use Chef Tony's Miracle Blade III knife to open the
bag, or if misplaced, use your teeth.

Congratulations! It's chow time.

It worked like a charm. I ripped the contents of the bag
open and devoured it in seconds. I noticed it was devoid
of any marshmallow treats, but still, it was magically delicious.

Upon arriving home and seeing the pantry door open with
the empty bag on the floor, my mother shook her head in
disappointment. She didn't even yell at me. After all these
years, she was a beaten woman.

It wasn't until the following morning, with just Marcy
Catcollector and me in the house, that I noticed a grumbling in my stomach. This meant only one thing, I had to
go number two and quickly!

I got up and ran to the door. Catcollector didn't move.
She wasn't asleep, just lazy. She made Mr. Couch Potato
Head look active. I pranced around making sure she heard
me. Still, there was no movement. I whined until I couldn't
hold it any longer, and pooped on the floor. Not of the normal Baby Ruth variety but a mud pie.

The smell immediately overwhelmed the room forcing my dog-sitter in charge to get vertical and clean up after me. She wasn't happy. But truth be told, she was responsible.

After completing this chore, and giving me an earful, she lay down again. Almost immediately, I felt the grumbling in my belly again. Could this be? So soon? I ran to the door. This time she noticed and opened it for me. A few steps out and my butt exploded. The deck now had a nice Bo deposit on it.

I wasn't allowed back into the house so I made my way onto the lawn. Here, I pooped some more. What was wrong with me?

After wiping and washing my paws, I was ready to return inside the house. I wasn't allowed to until a few hours later when my parents came home. Catcollector told them of my pooping escapades.

"I wonder what he got into?" my father asked.

"I really can't think of anything," my mother said as she searched her memory. "Unless the bag of cereal he ate yesterday was the bran cereal I bought for my father!"

"I didn't notice any bran cereal in the pantry. Are you sure?" Marcy asked.

"It was in a Ziploc bag."

Still trying to get a handle on the situation, Marcy looked for clarification. "Why was it in a Ziploc bag?"

Then, hit by an inspirational moment she answered her own question, "It was Mommy who put it in there, wasn't it?"

It sure was.

And the backyard had the poop to prove it.

CHAPTER 28

To Serve and to Protect

I couldn't decide.

Did she look like De Niro in *Raging Bull* or Rocky in any of the *Rocky* movies?

"Well, if you're going to press me, Moose, I'm going to go with the first Rocky, just before he asked Mick to cut him."

Moose looked shocked.

"Yeah, it's that bad," I said.

Moose had just received another beat-down from the neighborhood feline thug, Skittles.

I licked the tasty liquid from her face, doing my best to clean her up before my parents had a chance to see her. Maybe we could avert a visit to the vet's office, but even my surgical licks couldn't cover up Moose's swollen face.

My mother walked into the room and sensed something was amiss. She examined me—I was usually the one with issues—and then Moose.

A second later she yelled to my father, "Honey! Moose got into another fight!"

"Not again!"

"Yup. This one looks pretty bad. Get the car ready."

A bevy of activity followed and Moose was whisked away to the local place of healing. When she returned she had the requisite satellite dish around her neck and three bottles of pills.

Later that night, I sat down with a drugged-up Moose and reassured her all would be okay. I knew she was well past her cat boxing prime and now, in her older years, needed protection. I volunteered to even the score. I'm her big brother, isn't that one of my jobs?

Skittles was the neighborhood bully that all cats tried to steer clear of. Even some dogs dared not cross her path. She'd used Moose as a scratching post several times, and I vowed to end that practice.

Granted, I'm more of a lover than a fighter, unless I'm fighting over the last piece of pumpkin pie. Then I'd be willing to paw your eyes out, if I had to. But my tough talk about getting retribution for Moose was mostly false bravado.

Besides, I'd only encountered Skittles once in seven years, and from quite a distance at that, so I figured my chances of having to make good on my offer to Moose were pretty slim.

As luck would have it, the mysterious engines of fate brought Skittles and I together on a typical Georgia summer night: hot and humid without the hint of a breeze. The cicadas sang their song, creating a summer symphony as my mother and I enjoyed an evening stroll. My mother walked contentedly while I checked every tree, shrub, and mailbox for a semblance of critter activity.

We were approaching Skittles territory and I crossed the street to check if she'd been out that day. A strong odor lingered; she'd been out all right, and in this very spot as recently as just a few minutes ago. Adrenaline surged into my body. If I spotted her, what would it be, fight or flight?

No sooner had I smelled Skittles's evil odor than I looked up to see a big white fluff ball staring me down from twenty feet away. It was her, and she looked mean.

Rumor had it she was the meanest cat to tread the lands of Atlanta since the feline Fifi Sherman had put match to timber back in 1864 in a catnip-induced rage.

Skittles sat at the end of a driveway nearest the house. The only thing keeping me from her was a big SUV parked between us. This was my out, if I chose to cower instead of fight. I dug deep down, scratching for every last piece of courage I had. I decided to fight for my sister, damn it. She deserved it.

I made my move.

My mother was oblivious to the clash about to occur until it was too late. I was off like a bullet. That's fast. To her credit, she held on to the leash as long as she could, but after a few long, awkward strides, she was forced to let go lest she fall on her face.

I quickly advanced toward Skittles and was almost at her side when fate intervened. The retractable restraint— big, blue, and sturdy—jerked free from my mother's hands, skittered across the pavement, and wedged itself under the SUV's tire. I was jerked backward a mere foot from my target, who paused just long enough to shoot me a smug look before fleeing into the bushes.

I pulled against the leash with all of my strength, all the while yelling at Skittles, "You want a piece of this? C'mon. It's go time, kitty kat. Let's see how tough you are when you ain't facing a defenseless fur ball on social security." My mother tugged at the leash, which was wedged tightly under the SUV's tire, and hissed at me to shut up. I wouldn't. Adrenaline coursed through my veins as I shouted threat after threat, enjoying my tough-guy role.

It was nearly 11 p.m. and I knew my hollering was disturbing the neighbors, but I wasn't finished telling Skittles what I thought of her. It was at this point that a patrol car came up the street. It slowed and then stopped in front of the house where we were. I continued to shout.

The officer shined a floodlight on me, then on my mother, who was on her hands frantically trying to free my leash from the tire of the SUV.

"Oh, shit," my mother said when the floodlight hit her.

The police car's flashing blue lights turned on.

"Raise your hands and get away from the vehicle," a voice blared from the vehicle's loudspeaker.

My mother got up, raised her hands, and walked into the light.

As she did, the lights in Skittles's house turned on. In fact the lights of several other homes came on. There were big things going on in little Butler Creek and a few fortunate neighbors had front-row seats.

"I'm just trying to free my dog. His leash got stuck under this tire. He was chasing a cat," my mother yelled toward the cruiser.

The officer assessed the situation, quickly deciding that my mother was not a threat.

With all this excitement I continued to bark, not only at Skittles but also at the officer.

This was my first encounter with a real-life police officer. I wanted to show that I was a tough dog, one that could handle himself, just in case, you know, there was ever an opening in the K9 unit. I'd be a perfect police dog, I love donuts.

"Can you please make your dog stop barking?" the officer asked as he approached my mother.

"No."

"Why not?"

"Because he doesn't want to."

"Can't you make him?"

"No."

"Is he not your dog?"

"He is. But he won't listen to me."

"Have you tried dog training?"

"It wouldn't help. He's stubborn. Besides he'd never give up his control."

I continued to bark with excitement.

This was my kind of night. Start off with a little chase, add some confrontation, and top it off with a heap of humiliation. My job was to make sure the serving size was big enough to satisfy my mother.

I could make out several heads in the neighbors' windows.

"I'll be right back," said the officer as he walked toward his patrol car. My mother took the opportunity to finally force the leash free from under the SUV. I continued to bark.

After searching for a minute in his car, the officer found what he was looking for. When he emerged, I smelled something in the air. Something good. The guy in blue had a treat. I ran to him and wagged my tail.

"Does your dog bite?" he asked my mother.

"No."

"And you're sure he's your dog?"

"Yes."

Clearly this guy had seen the *Pink Panther* movies a few times.

"Here ya go, buddy," he said as he gave me a peanut butter–flavored cracker.

I swallowed it whole. That's good stuff.

Reaching into his pocket for another treat the officer asked, "What's his name, ma'am?"

"Bo"

"Bo. Sit!"

Oh, this was too easy. So I sat . . . and got another treat. Just to humiliate my mother further, I gave the officer my paw and then rubbed my head against his leg. It wasn't something I normally did, but it just seemed to work in this situation.

"Ma'am, he's a sweet dog and quite trainable. In fact it seems he's partially trained already. I'd suggest you take a basic obedience class with him. It will do wonders for your relationship with him plus it will keep you from embarrassing situations like this."

"He only sat for you because he wanted that treat. Either that or he just wanted to make me look like a horse's behind. At this point I'm not sure what motivates him more."

"Dogs don't have bad intentions. In fact there are no bad dogs, but there are bad owners."

"You'd change your mind if you lived with this one."

My mother was subconsciously rubbing the arm that had been jerked wildly just moments before. Noticing this, the officer asked, "Would you like me to give you a ride to your house?"

"I'd really appreciate that. My arm really hurts."

We piled into the back of the police cruiser as people watched from their windows. It probably looked as if we were being arrested. I couldn't wait to hear the gossip at the subdivision's pool the next day.

Once we got to our house the kind officer let us out of the car. He reiterated to my mother that she should really strive to train me.

Before he drove off he said, "Good boy. Bo is such a good boy!"

As his lights disappeared into the night my mother turned to me and yelled, "Bad boy. Bo is such a bad boy!"

BAD TO THE BONE

When I told Moose the story the next day, she brought me a dead field mouse to thank me for chasing Skittles. I felt wrong keeping it all for myself, but I knew exactly what to do with it.

I put it on my mother's bed. It's the least I could do for upsetting her.

CHAPTER 29

Money Matters

"I just don't get it. Where the heck is all our money going?" my father wondered aloud. It was the same comment he made at the end of every year during his annual exercise of downloading all the transactions from his online bank and credit card accounts and reconciling the family's net worth. Every year he came to an amount less than he had hoped for. Apparently he wasn't factoring in the goodwill I accounted for.

I was never too worried with his proclamation, mainly because I knew he always funded my Roth IRA before his own. That's the way it should be; you look out for your kids first. It's not selfish to expect to be able to travel and eat soft dog food in retirement. I knew he'd figure a way to make it happen.

This year's announcement seemed firmer, and as it turned out, the beginning of his search for every penny spent in the household. After days of poring over financial data he emerged with a sorry tale.

ATM fees, overdraft charges, and my weekly case of Frosty Paws were all singled out as wasteful expenditures that must be stopped. Other, bigger dollar items were also highlighted. Most notably the dollars spent on home improvement projects and dinners out. Worst of all, nights spent cruising

The Seven Habits of Highly Effective Dogs

1. *Eating*   Without proper nutrition, you can't function effectively. Please Google Maslow Mastiff's Hierarchy of Needs.

2. *Begging*   See Eating above.

3. *Sleeping*   No one likes a droopy eyed canine unless he's named Huckleberry Hound. Studies show bad decisions are made when you've logged less than 15 hours of sleep in a day.

4. *Peeing*   Just try to close a business deal with your back paws crossed; kidney stones develop if you don't let it go.

5. *Protecting*   What's yours is mine, what's mine is mine.

6. *Chasing*   When you see what you want, go for it.

7. *Cuddling*   Everyone needs love, regardless of what they say.

Curiosity is just going to kill you at a young age.

the aisles of PetSmart were going the way of pay telephones on a street corner.

He sat the family down and dictated the new fiscal policy in the house. It went something like this: if you want something other than the basics of food, clothing, or shelter, you have to find a way to pay for it outside of the family's normal income stream. It was that simple.

My immediate thought went to what I could sell on Craigslist; my unused dog bed, a rarely used Kong, and maybe even my parents if someone would have them. I knew that wouldn't garner much cash but I knew I would have to do something; my midnight snacking was at risk. But I wasn't the only being inconvenienced.

My mother objected, too. She had bigger things on her mind. "What about the shabby carpet upstairs? We can't live in the house with that. It smells really bad and looks horrible, too."

"I'm all for replacing it, you just need to find a way to pay for it," my father retorted.

He was dealing from a position of power since my mother was not working for monetary gain at the time. Truth be told, she was actually working for non-monetary gain, and this was driving some of the old man's anxiety.

Earlier that year, my mother and her friend opened a ladies only gym. They took cash out of their pockets and invested it in the venture they would call Girls Just Wanna Be Fit. Unfortunately for the new partners, they found out that really wasn't the case. Had they opened up Girls Just Wanna Be Eating we would all be living in million-dollar homes today.

I was invited to the gym several times to watch my mother work. After several such visits I now understood why my mother would mutter "change stations" in her sleep. Every forty seconds, for ten hours each day, there was a recording that said, "Change stations." That's . . . hold on let me get my calculator . . . ten hours times sixty minutes times sixty seconds divided by . . . let's just say that's a lot of times a day. So I could understand, with this ingrained in her mind, that she would mumble it a few times at night. Copper and I used it as our cue to roll over. That way we wouldn't get bed sores.

But the business venture put pressure on the family's financial resources right up until the day the gym was sold a year later. It turned out, my mother and her friend weren't the only ones who didn't know girls don't wanna be fit.

But at this point, the fitness experiment's end game wasn't yet in view. So my father continued with his edict.

Throwing a bone of sorts to my mother, he said, "I do think we need to finish the garden outside by putting up the retaining wall, so we'll spend money for that. But as for the carpet, you are on your own."

It wasn't much of a concession to my mother, or me since I was already in the midst of Frosty Paws withdrawal, but it was something. The new garden would be a great place to dig, considering the loose topsoil and all. I also knew I would be invited for the ride to the home improvement center to pick up the bricks when it was time. So it wasn't all bad.

The day to retrieve the bricks finally arrived; I called shotgun and my mother and I took off in my father's truck.

Once at the store, she headed to a special area for outside materials. To get at the bricks, my mother had to back up the pickup truck between two rows of pavers, bricks, and stones. I covered my eyes with my paws, wishing my father were there to navigate the gauntlet, for my mother's driving record going forward was pretty poor. I didn't even want to venture a guess as to how bad it would be going backward. But, to her credit she managed to back it up and angle the truck into the spot where two young workers could easily load up the vehicle. As they were doing this, she went in to pay the bill. I sat in the passenger seat supervising their work.

"Quit the chit-chatting and pick up the pace. This isn't a sewing circle you know," I growled at the teens.

With about half the truck loaded, a yellow-looking robot with a load of bricks came cruising toward me. It looked as if it were going to run right into the truck, but before it did, it lowered its boom and left a pallet of rocks right outside the truck's door. Whew! I thought for sure those bricks were going to be dumped on my father's precious rig, but more important, me.

Then my mother returned. She gave a slip of paper to the young gentlemen and began to drive off. As she pulled out, we both noticed a horrible screeching noise—it sounded worse than a dewclaw scratching a chalkboard. I thought my brain was going to explode.

What was it? An alien invasion or a new diabolical device used by the military to train dogs? No. It was the sound of the truck as it scraped against the pallet of rocks that had been placed on the ground during my mother's absence.

I looked at my mother. She had her "O" face on. The "Oh, sheet" face.

She stopped the truck and quickly got out to examine the damage. As she rounded the front corner of the truck to see what had happened, her jaw dropped. The two young workers followed and had the same expression. I couldn't see the damage because I couldn't stick my head out of the closed window. Let me just say whoever invented manual cranks for car windows was not a dog lover. I was forced to listen from inside the cabin.

"Wait until your husband sees that," one of the customers

remarked. Good point and one I was curious about, too, especially after the financial lecture we had received.

My mother immediately sprang into action, demanding that the store take responsibility for the damage. The workers tried to deny it, but if there's something I've learned about my mother, she doesn't give up if she feels she is in the right, or for that matter, even if she is wrong.

Moments later she was bending the ear of the store manager as he looked over the damage. He was quick to agree with my mother and had her fill out a claim form. I was still anxious to hear what my father would say.

As my mother drove us home, I could see the wheels spinning in her head. Hmmm, what kind of tale was she going to weave? There really wasn't anything wrong with what she did, and I suspected the claim would have his truck back to normal condition in no time. But there was something about the look in my mother's eyes that told me something was up. I just couldn't put my paw on exactly what.

When we got home, my father unloaded the truck. When he finally saw the deep scratches in the door, my mother told him the story of what occurred. My father wasn't happy, but he realized accidents happen and there wasn't much he could do about it. Unbeknownst to my father, she'd left out one tiny detail.

A month later, a crew of strangers arrived at the house. They stripped the upstairs of the old carpet and installed a new one in its place. By the time my father got home that evening, the upstairs floor had been totally redone.

Why my mother found the need to replace the carpet is beyond me. It has years of great smells already built in. A new one just means I'm going to have to pee and roll on it until it's worn in. I don't think I'll ever truly understand her.

I wasn't the only one.

My father noticed the new carpet at once. "I thought we agreed that we weren't going to buy anything unless we found a way to pay for it ourselves?"

"Don't worry; I have a way to pay for it."

He was surprised, "Really? Did you sell something on eBay?"

"No."

"Then where did the money come from?"

"You'll be so proud of me! Remember how your truck got all scratched up? Well Home Depot sent us a check to get it fixed."

"What?"

"I filed a claim. The check came this week and that's what I used to pay for the carpeting."

My father was speechless.

My mother continued, "You didn't say there was a certain way to come up with the money. You just said, find a way and you wouldn't care. Well I found a way."

By my mother's logic, he had already resigned himself to driving around in a scratched-up truck, so the new carpet was really a freebie.

I couldn't wait to see which vehicle she's going to crash to get that dining room set she has her eye on. And my father won't be able to say a thing.

She's just being fiscally responsible.

CHAPTER 30

Deliverance

It was their thirteen-year anniversary and my father was about to receive the best anniversary present a man could ever want. What was the gift?

Nothing.

How can "nothing" be a gift? When it's given in a make-believe box, wrapped with a make-believe bow, and delivered under the right circumstances.

You see, after thirteen years of marital bliss, and thirteen years to the day my father vowed his undying love for his new bride, he received nothing to commemorate the day from my mother. Not a card, not a kiss, not even an acknowledgment. Not until he called her on it.

He woke on that anniversary morning, went to his secret card hiding place, and scribbled some words on a card before going downstairs to give it to my mother. She sat on the couch, looking confused.

"What's this?" she asked.

"A card because I love you," he said as he bent down to give her a kiss.

I could tell by her expression that she wasn't expecting a card, or the flowers he quickly produced from their hiding place moments later.

When she opened the card that read Happy Anniversary, it dawned on her that she had forgotten her own wedding day.

Once my father realized she didn't have a card ready to give him he asked, "You forgot, didn't you?"

"Uhmm yes," she said sheepishly.

Score one for the old man.

Later that day my mother rushed out to get him a card. In it she wrote, "Happy 14th Anniversary! I love you!! xoxoxoxo."

Nice sentiment, and potentially a save of a bad situation, if only she had gotten the length of her own marriage correct. For my old man, this anniversary was the gift that kept on giving.

My father's alter gift-giving ego had shown up for this occasion, much to my mother's chagrin. Not only had he remembered their anniversary with a card and flowers, he had planned a special weekend getaway.

Normally I wouldn't take much interest, but this year I was specifically asked to join the family!

The surprise destination was the Highlands. I was so excited.

I wondered whether my father had won the lottery or something. Maybe this was my chance to meet my hero, Agent 049. You know, Sean Connery's dog. Even if I didn't, I couldn't wait to meet a few of the local Scottish terriers and make fun of their accents.

I practiced in the mirror, "I pees an' I pees til I can' pees na mahr!"

Ahh, the Highlands. I couldn't wait. Until, I found out it wasn't the Highlands located in Scotland, but rather Highlands, North Carolina.

Regardless, I planned to make the most of it.

After a three-hour car ride in the backseat—my mother had called shotgun—we arrived at our destination; a dog-friendly bed-and-breakfast. The white colonial inn stood out against the golden leaves in this heavily treed area. The cool, pollution-free air displaced the Atlanta smog from my lungs. Quite simply, it was spectacular.

We checked in and were accompanied to a wildlife-themed room. A large bed took up most of the space, and there was a small dog bed in the corner. I appreciated the effort, but they didn't really expect me to sleep on that, did they?

It was a perfect afternoon to go hiking on the local trails, and we all agreed we were up for the walk. The only question was which path to take.

"Do you want to do an easy trail or an intermediate one?" my father asked.

"Let's do the easy one. We don't want to wear ourselves out on the first day," my mother said.

I was all for an easier walk. My legs were still stiff from the three-hour car trip. Besides, I hadn't really exercised lately and was a bit out of shape. With that said, I was still in better shape than either of my parents.

A ten minute car ride later and we were at the head of a well-marked hiking trail. Unfortunately, it had a big sign, a very big sign: "Closed."

"This is where we start," my father declared.

"But why does it say 'Closed'?" my mother asked, a bit worried.

"The innkeeper said they had some mudslides because of all the rain they received recently. If we get to an area that looks dangerous, we'll just turn around. It's not a big deal. It's the easy trail."

I strained on the leash to get us moving up the trail. And with that last bit of encouragement, we were on our way.

The trail was a cross between brown dirt, rocks, and

leaves. On the inside edge, the rocks of the hills protruded out, while on the outer side one could see the farmland below. It was worthy of a picture. If only we hadn't forgotten our camera.

As we climbed the trail, I was thrilled to pick up all the messages left by canine tourists. I ran from side to side to check each one. I quickly came to love the Canadian dog tourists. They were so nice and all of their pees ended in "eh." That's one of the fun things about traveling, isn't it? You get to meet butts you wouldn't encounter at home, and get to share your own story for all to smell.

As our slow assent to the clouds continued, the trail took us deeper and deeper into wooded terrain. I couldn't see the farmland below anymore, but I didn't care, the messages were just as abundant. Every once in a while we would spot a marking on a tree, indicating we were on the right path.

My father wheezed with every step.

"This sure doesn't feel like an easy trail. I'm winded," he observed, "but I bet it evens out in a little bit."

We continued on.

A minute later my mother spoke up. "My sneakers are starting to hurt."

"Let me guess, they're new."

"Yes."

"Why do you always buy new sneakers before we go somewhere? You know they're going to bother you."

"The other ones are dirty."

Even though she only bought one pair a year, it always seemed she bought them before going on a trip. That's fine and all, but still, you'd think she'd break them in before going on a hiking trip. I know I always make sure to break in my paw pads before doing any serious walking. That said, this walk was tiring me out, too.

Fortunately for everyone involved, it wasn't long before we got to the lookout. We milled around, my parents alternating between taking in the view and sitting on the bench.

We started to walk back when we came to a cross in the path. It's a junction my parents hadn't noticed when they came upon the lookout. Instead of going straight, they took the left trail.

I yelled, "You're going the wrong way. It's this way!"

They didn't listen. A quick yank of the leash and I was soon following them down the wrong path.

It had taken us forty-five minutes to get to the lookout, and we were an hour into our walk back down the chosen path before my parents began to suspect we'd gone the incorrect way.

It was a tree that had fallen across the trail that clued them into the problem.

"I'd remember if we crossed this. We're definitely going the wrong way," my father finally said to my mother.

In the distance, and through the trees, I could barely make out our car. We had walked several miles the wrong way, and now out of sheer luck, we could get to the car.

"We'd better turn around," he said.

I turned, did my best pointer impression, and pointed toward the car.

"Bo, stop clowning around and let's go," scolded my father, who once again tugged at my leash as we retraced our steps up the path. Our "easy" walk turned into a four-hour hike, and the sad part was, we were only half way done.

My mother begged my father to leave her. She assured him they would be able to find her body in the spring. But he wasn't going to let her take the easy way out.

By the time we emerged from the trail, it was almost dark. What was supposed to be a quick, warm-up walk for the weekend turned into the only one we would take. We were sore and exhausted for the next two days.

Upon coming back to the inn, my father told the innkeeper, "That trail was a lot harder than it says."

"Which side did you go in on?" the innkeeper asked.

"We went in the one that said closed."

"Oh, that explains it. That side is the hard trail." Pointing at a map, he said, "The easy side starts here."

Much like most of their lives, my parents had taken me on the path more difficult.

Part Three
This End Up

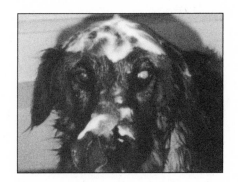

CHAPTER 31

Eat. Spit. Be Happy.

It was late October and my mother was hosting the monthly Bunco get together with some of the neighborhood ladies.

To the uninitiated, Bunco is a dice game similar to Yahtzee, but exclusively played by women. As far as I can tell, it's primarily used as an excuse to stick husbands with the responsibility of caring for the kids (and pets) for the evening while the wives get a chance to socialize with each other. The most important aspect of this monthly ritual is that no husband is allowed within earshot of the festivities. As a male dog, even I am banned. As much as I've tried, no amount of cajoling will get my sister Copper to open her muzzle about what goes on, either. It's a secret society, equivalent to the secret handshake we dogs employ.

Haven't heard about the handshake?

Of course not, it's a secret.

At least every male in the neighborhood now understood the humiliation a dog feels when forced out of the house because company comes over.

My father and I received the equivalent of a door opening and a high heel pushing our tushes out the door. We were left to our own devices.

My father decided to kill time by going Halloween costume shopping, not for him but for me. Although I have a closet full of suitable attire, there's an unwritten rule that one doesn't break: *Though shall not double-dip on a previous year's costume.* That's the only reason I could come up with as to why we had to go shopping every year to get me something goofy to wear. Truth be told, it didn't have to be goofy, it could be any Disney character. The upside was that at least I got to go with him for a little male bonding, and that I would get a chance to visit an all-you-can-eat sunflower buffet.

Cruising down the busy street, my father stroked my chest, wondering out loud the mean things the ladies were saying about men generally and him specifically. I wondered about more important things, like what kind of leftovers would be available when I got home.

Our first and only stop was at the Super TarJay. My father grabbed his wallet and headed inside the store. Left alone in the truck, the opportunity I had been looking for arose.

Strewn about the truck's floor were sunflower seeds; they were everywhere. If one didn't know better, they would have thought a bird feeder exploded in the truck. Too good to pass up, I started to dine on the finest sunflower seeds known to man. I ate until I was full, leaving only a handful of seed carcasses untouched.

By the time my father had finished his shopping trip, I had finished my meal and repositioned myself on the seat of the truck, the picture of canine innocence.

Grinning from ear to ear he said to me, "Bo, you are going to love this! I think this is the best costume I've ever gotten you." The look on his face and the excitement in his voice set off the warning bells in my head—I would soon be humiliated.

After a quick stop at the gas station we headed home, arriving just as the Bunco party was winding down. Seeing an opportunity to get some laughs, my father rushed me into the basement where I was forced to sit still while he dressed me in my costume. I couldn't make out what the outfit was but noted it was dark in color. It was either dark blue, dark red, dark green, dark (fill in the blank here). I couldn't tell because, hey, I'm color-blind. The pièce de résistance was some kind of hat he put on my head. He stepped back and looked me up and down. I guessed from his deep belly laugh that he wasn't laughing with me.

Despite my protests, he escorted me up the basement steps, pushed me through the door, quickly closing it behind me.

I was now in a roomful of chattering women. Before I could plot my escape, one of the women caught sight of me and snorted with laughter. On cue, the entire party turned at once, their laughs building into a crescendo. It's the sound Eddie Murphy must have heard from audiences worldwide . . . in the early years. The laughter continued unabated for five minutes, while I stood there, soaking in the humiliation like a sponge and listening to my father chuckle on the other side of the door.

What to do? What to do?

Well, if at a Bunco party, do what the Bunkonians do. I shook off my embarrassment and did what I do best—begged for food. A little pleading here, some paw giving there and I was scoring some major caches of cheese and crackers. I guess these ladies will allow you into their club as long as you look silly enough.

Eventually the ruckus calmed down, and the ladies left. By all accounts the night was a success; for my mother because no one left with food poisoning, for my father because he found me a costume, and for me because I was bursting at the seams from the leftovers.

While cleaning, my mother inadvertently knocked a large

serving spoon onto the floor. Although I was already full, I seized it between my two paws and licked it clean. Lick by lick, the reflection on the spoon became clearer. When I finished, what I saw astounded me. Reflected back at me was . . . Darth Vader. I, Bo Hoefinger, was dressed up like the Dark Lord of the Sith. My old man was right, he had truly outdone himself.

Little did I know the construction of the Death Star had begun without my command.

It would be three days before I had my next bowel movement, notable only because I'm a one-a-day bomber. In addition to being late, I had difficulty controlling it when I finally did have to go, which resulted in an accident in the middle of the kitchen floor. Moments later my mother came upon the scene.

Upon close inspection, she noticed something peculiar about my poo. After bagging my stool, she marched downstairs to have a discussion with my father. I followed her.

"Uhmm, is there something you want to tell me?" she asked him.

Seeing that trouble was looking for him, he replied, "Yeah, I love you."

"Did you give Bo sunflower seeds to eat?"

"Sunflower seeds? No, of course not. You know I like them too much."

Holding the bag of crap in the air, she asked, "Then how do you explain that his poop has sunflower shells in it?"

My father sat there for a moment, chewing at his lower lip thinking of a way to answer the question with minimum fallout. It wasn't his fault, but he knew the finger pointing was coming his way. Finally he said, "Hmmm . . . I wonder if he ate some when I took him shopping for his costume on Tuesday?"

Sarcastically my mother retorted, "Yeah, I wonder."

After a moment of silence and a glare that's turned men into stone, my mother said, "Do me a favor and don't give him any more seeds." And with that she took the bag of poop and delivered it to the garbage container outside. My father sat there dumbfounded, wondering how he had just gotten blamed for me taking a dump in the middle of the kitchen.

I awoke the following day, feeling a bit off as my mouth was killing me and I couldn't stop drooling. It was like someone was taunting me with a big, juicy steak that they wouldn't let me have. But here's the thing, they weren't. I was just drooling for no reason at all. To top it off, I was having difficulty breathing.

I didn't want to do anything, not even water the plants.

It didn't take long for my father to notice. Spotting the big wet stain where I slept, my father stuck his fingers in my mouth to see if there was anything in there. He found nothing. Then his hands moved to under my chin where a growth the size of a tennis ball bulged out.

I smelled the fear overwhelm him. Although he didn't dare say it to my mother, he feared the lump was cancer. It was time for yet another ride to the Cobb Emergency Vet Clinic.

On the ride over, my mother sat in the backseat with me, holding my head in her lap and telling me everything would be fine. I wanted to tell her, "Move over, you're crowding me," but I didn't want to hurt her feelings.

Once we arrived, the technician checked me in and immediately carried me to one of the examining rooms. My parents filled out a mountain of paperwork.

I have to admit I was a bit concerned. I'd never had so much difficulty breathing, even when my father had me pinned underneath the covers. And what was with the drool? If this is what Cujo had to deal with, I can see why he lost his marbles and attacked people (and cars).

My parents finally finished the paperwork and arrived in the room accompanied by the emergency vet. She immediately focused on the growth below my face and gave a grave assessment of my situation.

She indicated that in dogs my age, cancer could grow rapidly near the saliva gland. Bracing my parents for what may lay ahead, she pointed out I was a perfect candidate. You know what I thought I'd be a perfect candidate for? Dog of the Year, not this. I admit I was scared. After the doctor sedated me, she ordered X-rays and a biopsy, then aspirated the growth. The Death Star was just about complete.

She told my parents to come back later in the evening.

Upon their return, the tech escorted them into an examining room where I and the emergency vet waited. I was a bit groggy from the anesthesia, but I was very happy to see my folks.

The mood in the room was dark.

The vet started somberly, "As you know, he was pretty stubborn about letting anyone look inside his mouth."

My parents nodded their heads simultaneously in agreement.

"Once I had him sedated I was able to fully examine the area underneath his tongue. Let me ask you, did he get into anything recently that may have caused a cut or an infection?"

My father was quick to speak up. "No."

"Well, I found this embedded in a cut under his tongue," she said, holding up a sunflower shell high against the light. "Do you know where he might have gotten something like that?"

My mother swiftly turned to my father. "See. I told you

that you can't leave him in the car with all those seeds lying around!"

I guess I wasn't the only one she was quick to turn on when something was done wrong. She continued while alternately looking at the vet and glaring at my father. "Yes, Doctor. We think he got into some sunflower seeds. My husband insists on spitting them onto the floor of his truck. Bo was left alone in the truck and must have eaten some."

The vet responded, "He really shouldn't be eating that. It's not good for him, plus it will make him constipated."

No kidding.

The doctor continued with her medical dissertation. "Anyway, the seed caused a big infection and abscess near his saliva gland. That was the reason he was drooling and having difficulty breathing. We've aspirated the growth and will be sending it to pathology for testing just to be sure, but I'm pretty confident he'll be fine."

Did I hear that correctly? I'm going to be fine? My parents confirmed what I heard. Their faces lit up with joy. "He's going to be fine!"

I was sent home with a pawful of medications for my infection and under strict rules to get some rest. Like these days they have to tell me that.

I can't believe I was nearly taken out by a sunflower seed.

On the way to the car I looked up into the sky and saw a large explosion. It was the Death Star.

CHAPTER 32

The Old Shoe

"It smells like an old shoe in here," said the acupuncturist as she leaned over me.

I hoped she was referring to my father, but I suspect it might have been directed at me.

This new care regimen was part of a holistic health kick my parents were on. You see, I had been struggling to walk up and down the two flights of stairs in the house, and I hadn't been able to climb up on the bed for quite some time. It didn't help that the bed was so high that on cloudy days you couldn't see the top.

Admittedly, it's no fun getting old. Well, that's only partially true. Receiving the white glove treatment from my parents did have its benefits. More treats, more car rides, and not having to walk up that huge hill in the neighborhood were the upside. And as for gaining access to the bed; I had a free pass on the Daddy Express. The great thing about it was that it ran on my schedule. Other than that, old age sucks.

Half the time I can't even remember where I buried the car keys.

My parents signed me up for acupuncture to help with my achy joints. When I went for my first appointment I really didn't know what to expect. After being given a nice blanket to lie on, my parents sat down on the floor next to me. Concerned for my well-being, I noticed they held each other's hand as they petted me.

Then a holistic healer came in with a fishing tackle box, only this one was loaded with long, thin needles rather than lures. These needles were nothing like I'd become accustomed to. They were so thin, they weren't threatening. If used in battle I'd surmise it would take several hundred to bring a pug to its knees. I sat back and relaxed.

Soon enough the holistic healer pulled the first pin out of its container and, whammo, stuck it smack dab in the middle of my forehead.

I looked like a unicorn.

Moments later, I had twenty pins sticking out of my body and the healer left the room. Every eight minutes, a technician would come in and turn each pin. Why? I suspected it was just to torture me.

At least my parents were there to support me. They took the opportunity to reminisce about all the fun times we had throughout the years. I was about to ask them, "Hey is this a wellness visit or a wake?" but was interrupted by the technician turning the tiny swords into my skin. After twenty-four minutes, a timer went off, and I was done like a Thanksgiving turkey with its pop-up thermometer fully extended.

After we got home, I didn't notice a difference in my ability to traverse the stairs. Each step was still hard on the knees and the hips. Plus now I had a real hankering for Chinese food.

Even so, my parents were intent on continuing with the treatments.

On my second visit as a canine-shaped pin cushion, my father and I had time to kill while waiting in the examination room. In there, they had a paw touch screen where you could dial up information about canines and kitties. One of the features of this device allowed me to calculate how old I was in human years.

My father held me up as I punched in the particulars:

Years: one five <enter>

Weight: between 50–100 lbs <enter>

Health: average <enter>

Appearance: drop dead gorgeous <enter>

I clicked on CALCULATE AGE.

"You are . . . 99 canine years old"

Wow, ninety-nine! I didn't feel a day over ninety-five. It must be all that Dannon yogurt I've eaten over the years.

I'll be honest; I couldn't wait to turn one hundred so I could see my face on a jar of Smuckers and hear Willard Scott try to pronounce my last name on TV.

Shortly thereafter, my father took me to a room, where my favorite acupuncturist stabbed me with twenty-one pins. That made me wonder, did they forget one last time? If not, why did I get an extra one this time?

And where was this happy ending I always read about?

Surprisingly, after the third and then the fourth sessions, my hip and back started feeling better. I was able to get up on the bed with minimal help and my father didn't have to carry me up the stairs anymore. It was a miracle. I was a believer in the alternative medicine movement.

I couldn't wait to try some shark cartilage for my bad breath.

But good times never seem to last. A few days after my last acupuncture appointment, I began to feel ill. I was nauseous, dizzy, and couldn't control my bowels. It's as if I'd eaten too much of my mother's cooking while riding a non-stop Tilt-A-Whirl.

I feared the end was near.

My parents whisked me off to my second home, the vet's office.

There, the vet determined that I had geriatric vestibular syndrome. He said I had all its symptoms: a loss of balance, an adorable head tilt, rapid eye movements, along with the nausea and loss of bowel control.

Let's face it, when the name of a disease you have begins with the word *geriatric* you know you're no longer classified as a spring chicken.

Aside from the disturbing name, also worrisome was that its cause was unknown and there was no cure. That's not a good combination in a disease you have. It didn't look good for me.

That is, until I heard the good news. As quickly as this disease appears, it goes away, usually after two to three weeks.

When I heard that, I threw up with joy. On the living room rug, the kitchen floor, and the bedroom carpet.

But the humiliation of this disease was not yet complete. Since my mother didn't want to leave me outside to pee when the urge hit, or want to clean up after me inside the house after I had an accident, she came up with a solution. She bought me . . . doggie diapers. Now I could just pee and poop in my pants at will.

Who does she think I am, Larry King?

The first size she tried on me was too small; I had a little junk in my trunk—I wasn't exercising a lot. After they fit me with a properly sized diaper, I relaxed. Even though I was self-conscious of my appearance, I felt confident I wouldn't get yelled at for peeing in my own pants.

My parents took turns caring for me until my illness ran its course. My father carried me up and down the stairs and lifted me into bed, while my mother made sure to give me my medication. They took care of my every need. It was a team effort to get me back on all four paws, an effort that strengthened our already strong bonds.

Even after my recovery, there were lingering effects to the caring of an old friend. At night my parents would sit close together on the couch and watch me as I lay in front of the fireplace. They made sure I was comfortable as they spoke softly to each other.

They realized they were getting older, too. Much like me, they had become wiser about the important things in life and began to cherish every moment more with me, and each other.

I knew my recent health issues worried them, but I knew I'd be around for a while longer. I just wished I had a way to make them feel better.

If only I had a pin I could jam in their foreheads.

Epilogue

I hope you're not expecting a heart-wrenching letter from one of my parents to end this book, and by extension my life. There will be no statements like, "Bo took his final breath and fell off Rainbow Bridge on his way to meet his maker." Blah, blah, blah.

Nope. Not going to happen because I'm still typing away at the tender age of sixteen, and besides, I'm so nimble that falling off anything, other than my latest diet, isn't going to happen.

I have to admit I've grown quite a bit since that first encounter with my parents. From a know-it-all punk dog in a shelter, to one that enjoyed running free in suburbia, to the dog that enjoys just hanging with his family today. I achieved the "Dog Pound Dream."

After I finished writing this book, I couldn't help but be amazed at all the things my parents put me through. Let's be honest, nipple appointments and maxi pad bandages would have killed the average dog. My life should serve as a cautionary tale to any canine looking for adoptive parents. I can't stress enough, don't use your "human hook" to catch the first one you see, wait until you spot the right one before finalizing the deal.

What's amazed me the most about the process of writing this memoir has been how great it's been to relive the experiences. This book is a time machine allowing me to experience my life again. Little did I know this book, a present for my mother, was really a gift for me.

Although the family has grown older and grayer, we're all still doing fine. My father continues his work in the corporate world, although from a home office, and my mother still hasn't landed a full-time gig. My biggest decision these days is which of their offices to beg in. Moose continues to get clogged and Copper still farts while she walks. The more things change, the more they stay the same.

But there is a decidedly different tone in the house. It's not filled with cat chases and chaos, but instead with a soothing calm. We're all just enjoying each other.

Turns out the most important things in life were right under my big, wet nose.

Part Four
Bonus Material

Jackpot! —Geoff Edwards, game show host

Looks to me like there's 6 lbs of dog crap around here, and only a 5 lb book bag to fit it in. —Bo Hoefinger

Q and A with the Author

Q: *Why did you write this book?*
B: Because I could.

Q: *Let's try again. What did you want to accomplish by writing this book?*
B: To get more treats from my mother. I wrote this for her.

Q: *How did you learn to write?*
B: I wish I could tell you that there was a dramatic reason that caused me to be able to write, but I can't. All I know is that I've been typing away on keyboards since I was one. I must admit that I can't write with a pen, but hey look at Stephen Hawking, he isn't writing with a pen either and he's brilliant . . . and only a few points shy of my IQ.

Q: *What writers are your inspiration?*
B: Marmaduke and Clifford the Big Red dog. Their prose attained heights the average pug can't even imagine. Sometimes it reached as high as six feet.

Q: *Do you think it was fate that you ended up with your mother and father?*
B: I've wondered over the years whether my mother would have adopted me if my father hadn't chosen to pull that stunt during the holiday season all those years ago.

I know she's fond of monkeys, so it wouldn't have been out of the realm of possibilities for her to bring home a white-faced capuchin rather than a dog. Fortunately, there weren't any available when she showed up looking to adopt. Sure monkeys groom their owners, but unless a prospective owner is looking for an organ grinder, there's really not much of added value there.

Let's face it; they were lucky to get me. Fate intervened on their behalf, not mine.

Q: What's the deal with your mother not being able to find stable employment?
B: After her three hiring and firings early on, my parents decided that my father would work in the corporate world while Mother pursued the path to riches using her entrepreneurial skills.

She was all for it (who wouldn't be?) knowing that success was all but assured. You see there's this story she tells of an Indian boy, Sanjay, who read her palm in high school. He had approached her during gym class while they were learning to play tennis. As they waited in line to hit their next shot, he took her hand in his, turned it over, and told her the future: "You will be very wealthy someday. Plus you will live a long life."

So now she thinks she'll be wealthy, and an old bag to boot. You know and I know Sanjay was just trying to get under her sports bra, but why spoil her dream.

Q: What would you say to a young dog who wanted to become a writer?
B: I'd tell him/her to make sure to use an ergonomic chair. Otherwise your back is going to kill you. It also helps if the bathroom is on the same floor. That way you

don't have to pee in the corner of the room. Oh, and make sure to hook up with a great editor. She'll actually help you make sentences out of words you type.

Q: What advice would you give a dog trying to get adopted?
B: Put a call in to the Pitt/Jolie household. Those folks aren't shy about adopting.

Q: It seems you are a very creative dog. With all those thoughts going through your mind, how do you sleep at night?
B: Curled up, with my eyes closed.

Q: Dogs do a lot of twitching and yelping when they sleep. What are you dreaming about?
B: I can't speak for anyone else, but I'm usually chasing the Hamburgler. You'd think a burger that big would be slow and plodding. Even with those big shoes he wears, he's fast.

Q: If you were to become famous, how do you think it would affect you?
B: I can't see it affecting me. I would continue to be like any other dog; I'd put my fur suit on one paw at a time and go about my normal business. To all my friends, I'd continue to be Bobo from the block.

Q: Speaking about your normal business, what is your typical day like?
B: There aren't any hard fast rules that I follow except making sure that I'm by my owners' side when they wander into the kitchen. I don't want to waste any

opportunities to get me some extra human food. If I'm lucky a squirrel or chipmunk may be feeding in the "kill zone" and I'll get some exercise.

My day can be categorized fairly simply: sleep, pee/poop, eat, beg, nap, eat, beg, pee, sleep.

Q: What's your favorite color?
B: Gray. I'm color-blind.

Q: Is the moon really made out of cheese?
B: Common misconception, the answer is no. It's really made out of rawhide.

Q: Boxers or briefs?
B: Neither. I go commando.

Q: If a tree falls in the forest, can a dog hear it?
B: Sounds like a trick question . . . did I pee on it?

Q: What is your biggest fear?
B: That the inappropriate tape I made in my youth is released on the Internet.

Q: If you were to adopt a cat, what would you name it?
B: Lunch.

Q: What advice would you like to pass along to the young dogs reading this?
B: Floss after every meal.

Q: Anything else?
B: If your dog chow is delivered cold or soggy or just not in the way you are used to, whatever you do, don't send it back. Your owners will spit in it.

Q: If you could give the people of the world one message, what would it be?
B: Run, don't walk, to the nearest animal rescue group and adopt a loving canine in need (as a fallback position, adopt a cat). Only kidding, every house needs a cat, too. Not only will they save a life, but in the process they'll create a better one for themselves.

Q: What do you do when your folks leave the house?
B: Well, the first thing I do is make sure they've actually left. Sometimes they come right back after leaving the house, usually to get the car keys they forgot. This is the biggest mistake I see the young pups making these days, they get into their mischief too quickly.

After I'm sure they're gone for good, I'll head upstairs to the garbage pail. I'll flip the lid with my nose and see if it's full. If it is, I can usually pull out something to snack on. If the lid doesn't flip, I'll pull on the garbage bag lining that overhangs the can. It pulls the entire pail over and voilà, I get the "Golden Corral." It's an all you can eat buffet without the sneeze guard. If that doesn't work then I might bang my head against the container to knock it over. Nobody's around so I can make a ruckus without worrying about it.

I'll also bark at some squirrels and people throughout the day but the balance of the time is primarily spent sleeping. Oh yeah, I also work on my writing when I feel creative.

Q: If you could visit one place on this planet, where would it be?
B: Hamburg, Germany, unless the mythical Filet Mignon, France, truly exists. If so I'd head there with a super size bottle of ketchup.

Q: Okay, let's get political. What is your take on border security?
B: I'm not for it. Why? A dog should be free to roam this earth without limits. So many times I've been kept from a day of fun because of the fence. Sure it will keep the honest dog on the proper side of the line but a dog with bad intentions is going to get under it regardless . . . as I have proven countless times.

Q: What do you think about Iraq?
B: A rock? Well, there's a rock covering my favorite escape hole. I gotta be honest, I don't like it one bit.

Q: If you had a gun with two bullets in it and were confronted by Michael Vick, Sylvester the Cat, and Tweety Bird, whom would you shoot?
B: I'd shoot Michael Vick, twice.

Q: Thank you for your time. Do you have any last words for the readers out there?
B: I do. I'd like to thank all my dogs out there for supporting me. Stay real and make sure you don't pee on this book.

Interview with the Author's Parents

Q: *How has it been living with Bo?*
Mother: A true pleasure. He's the most well-behaved dog we ever adopted.
Father: Well that was true up until we adopted Copper, so I guess he's the second best behaved dog.

Q: *How many dogs have you owned?*
M: Just the two of them.

Q: *Bo seems pretty calm, how often does he wag his tail?*
F: Once in the morning and once in the evening.
M: We feel he's just trying to conserve energy so he can write.

Q: *Best Bo moment?*
F: The best Bo moment occurs when he returns after an escape. He comes to the front porch and barks to be let in. Although it's obnoxious, we're happy he's safe and home.

Q: *Worst Bo moment?*
F: When he's escapes for the entire night. Needless to say, we don't sleep very well.

Q: Same questions to you Mr. Bo's mom. Best and worst?

M: The best moment was when he growled at a stranger that knocked on my car window. At that point I knew he would protect the hand that fed him.

The worst moment, for him, occurred when we were walking on the shore of our local lake. Bo went to step on a rock by the lake's edge to get closer to the water. Unfortunately for him, it was a big leaf and not a rock. He ended up falling into the water and nearly drowning himself. I laughed so hard that I know his ego took a hit. He's still getting counseling for it to this day.

Q: If there were one thing Bo could tell you, what would you want it to be?

F: I'm curious about his first eleven months on this earth before we got him. What happened during that time to make him the dog he is today?

M: I'd want him to tell me why he constantly stares at me. He's incessantly doing this while I lay on the couch. I wish he could just tell me what the heck he wants so he can move on with his life.

Q: Final question . . . what's the story behind this series of stories?

F: The book was written as a Christmas present for Bo's mother. Instead of giving a gift that would soon be forgotten, the thought was to give her something that could be treasured forever. I think Bo met the challenge.

The Family Album

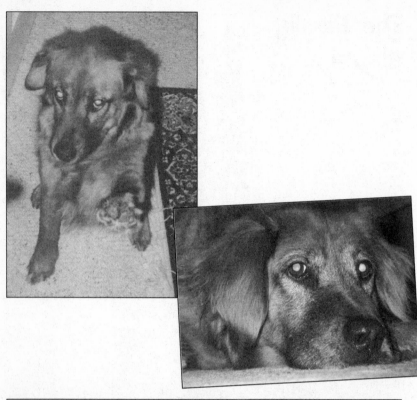

Bloopers!!

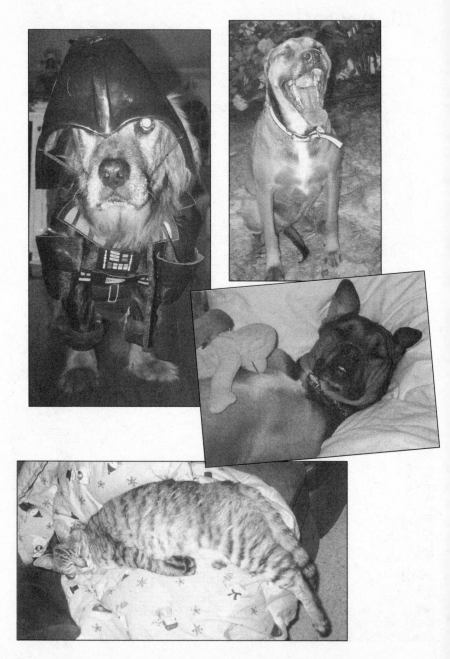

Acknowledgments

This book would not have been possible without a forward-thinking literary agent willing to take a chance on a four-legged, fur suit–wearing canine. Thank you, Barbara Poelle, for turning a Christmas gift into a published work of art. Your zany sense of humor, endless enthusiasm, and love of poop stories are truly appreciated. Hey, this poop's for you!

If every struggling writer could have an editor with the insight, patience, and fervor exhibited by Danielle Chiotti, there'd be a whole lot more books out there. Her ability to teach an old dog the new trick of not writing in passive language was truly inspirational. Thanks, Danielle, I think I'm ready for English 101 now!

I'd also like to recognize all of the wonderful people at Dogster.com. Thanks to founder Ted Rheingold for giving my parents the chance to blog on all things dog and to Anders Porter for making it a daily pleasure to inform readers on the latest dog happenings. I hope you realize the positive impact you've made in the lives of hundreds of thousands of pets and their owners. It is an honor to be associated with you.

I'd be remiss if I didn't thank Erin Brokovich. I don't know her, never met her, and probably couldn't smell her out in a crowded room, but it is her story that kept this dog writing and taking the needed steps forward on this project. Her life experiences showed me that things happen for a reason, and never to accept the word no.

And finally, I need to acknowledge my bladder. It doesn't accept the word no either, and it's telling me I have to go. So woof-bye for now!

Further Acknowledgments

This book would not have been possible without the support of my family and friends. Specifically Copper, whose memory of events is unequaled by any canine, my feline friend Moose, whose continued encouragement got me over the procrastination hump, IAMS Savory Sauce for keeping me motivated, [insert dog food name here]* for providing the essential vitamins and minerals to keep my brain functioning at the highest level and above all to the mother that adopted me. A more loving and kind soul has never been found.

*Product placement special. If Purina, Nature's Choice, Bil-Jac or any other pet food company would like to appear on this page please contact my agent. We can work out a deal to include your name in all future versions of this book in consideration for some treats.

About the Author

Bo Hoefinger is not the *New York Times* best-selling author of any books. An amazing insight into canine thinking led him to write this, his very first book.

A frequent contributor to local fence post 17, he continues his nonprofit work with the Beneath the Fence Association where he is the current chairman of the board. In his spare time he dabbles in knocking over garbage pails, barking uncontrollably, and generally being a helpful force around the house.

A native of Albany, New York, Bo now lives in Atlanta, Georgia, with his two sisters, Copper and Moose, and his two parents (who refuse to sign release papers allowing the publication of their names and pictures).